08-BZD-960

D0020241

GOD'S FAVORITES

JUDAISM,
CHRISTIANITY,
AND THE MYTH OF
DIVINE CHOSENNESS

MICHAEL COOGAN

Beacon Press
BOSTON

BEACON PRESS
Boston, Massachusetts
www.beacon.org

Beacon Press books
are published under the auspices of
the Unitarian Universalist Association of Congregations.

22 21 20 19   8 7 6 5 4 3 2 1

This book is printed on acid-free paper that meets the uncoated paper
ANSI/NISO specifications for permanence as revised in 1992.

Text design and composition by Kim Arney

Library of Congress Cataloging-in-Publication Data
Names: Coogan, Michael David, author.
Title: God's favorites : Judaism, Christianity, and the myth
of divine chosenness / Michael Coogan.
Description: Boston : Beacon Press, [2018] | Includes
bibliographical references and index.
Identifiers: LCCN 2017034551 (print) | LCCN 2017035257 (e-book) |
ISBN 9780807001950 (e-book) | ISBN 9780807001943 (hardcover : alk. paper)
Subjects: LCSH: Jews—Election, Doctrine of. | Election (Theology)
Classification: LCC BM613 (e-book) | LCC BM613 .C66 2018 (print) |
DDC 296.3/1172—dc23
LC record available at https://lccn.loc.gov/2017034551

*For Anne Steindorf
and James Coogan
with love*

CONTENTS

1
PRESUPPOSITIONS

*Yahweh your god chose you from all peoples on
earth to be his people, his treasured possession.*

—(Deuteronomy 7:6)

THROUGHOUT HISTORY, many groups have thought of themselves as divinely chosen, exhibiting what has been called a "holy
nationalism."[1] For the ancient Egyptians, the divine gift of the annual inundation of the Nile was proof they had been specially chosen; the Egyptians' neighbors, whom they called "the vile Asiatics,"
had clearly not been chosen, because their equivalent of the depend-
able Nile was unpredictable rain. Roman poets such as Virgil and
Ovid celebrated the divine plan that had brought Aeneas from the
burning ruins of Troy to Italy, from where eventually the emperor
Augustus would rule the Mediterranean world. But one ancient people's claim of divine chosenness has profoundly affected religious
and political self-identification for thousands of years, especially in
the West: the biblical view that God, the only God, has a favorite
people, the Israelites. Beginning in the early chapters of the book of
Genesis, chosenness is attached to individuals whom God supposedly
preferred—Abraham, Isaac, and Jacob—and is inherited by their
descendants, who have a special status because God chose their ancestors. Although in the pages of the Bible some of those originally
chosen eventually became excluded, the concept of chosenness continued to be applied to subgroups within the original chosen people.

Subsequently, still others applied the concept to themselves, asserting that those originally chosen had been divinely rejected because they had proven unworthy.

From antiquity to the present, the idea of being divinely chosen has had powerful and often pernicious effects. If only one group has been divinely chosen then others have not been, and that justifies subjugating them and taking their land. Such rationalization has been used repeatedly, in the most virulent forms of anti-Semitism, in the enslavement and even extermination of aboriginal peoples, and in the confiscation of land by force from those not chosen—be they Canaanites, Jews, Muslims, Africans, Native Americans, Palestinians, and too many others.

The concept of chosenness—often called *election*—is a difficult theological problem. Does God—the one god of Judaism, Christianity, and Islam—have favorites? Does God really prefer some individuals and groups over others? Are not his love and his mercy universal? Does God in fact choose at all? Philosophers and theologians have wrestled with this issue since biblical times.

In the first part of this book, I first analyze in detail competing and inconsistent claims of being divinely chosen by individuals and groups in ancient Israel and then turn to early Christian claims of being the new chosen people. My primary focus in the second part of the book is Western appropriations of the biblical concept of chosenness, especially by Americans and by Jewish and Christian religious Zionists.[2] Throughout, I suggest how my analysis could move us beyond contemporary tribalisms that are based on fundamentalist readings and misappropriations of ancient texts and that are rationalized by the myth of divine choice of some over others. I use the term *myth* both in its basic sense of a story with one or more deities as major characters as well as in its metaphorical sense of something that is not true.

I write not as a believer but as a modern biblical scholar, trained in the study of the Jewish and Christian scriptures. Let me explain what this means and why it is important. Since its final formation as a sacred text in the early centuries of the Common Era, the Bible was the preeminent authority for both Jews and Christians. What it said was simply the truth, because they believed it to be divine revelation—the words of God himself. In fact, it was considered not just the words of God but *the word* of God: both complete and completely accurate—*inerrant* is the term theologians use. Its status was therefore uniquely privileged, and thinkers had only to interpret it.

And interpret it they did: from Hillel and Philo of Alexandria to Rashi and Maimonides, from Paul and Origen to Aquinas and Erasmus and Luther, Jewish and Christian thinkers developed intricate and elegant systems of thought with the Bible at the center. But the privileged status of the Bible began to unravel in the late Renaissance and especially during the Enlightenment. The unraveling began with the rise of modern science, especially in the work of the astronomers Copernicus, Kepler, and Galileo, who argued that, despite what the Bible said, the earth was not the center of the universe. Further developments in biology, chemistry, and other sciences made it clear that the Bible's understanding of nature was often wrong, and its chronology was often inaccurate.

The Bible is not exactly the same book for Jews and for Christians. For Christians, it includes the New Testament, whereas for Jews it obviously does not. And although all of the books in the Jewish Bible are also in Christian Bibles, after the first seven books—from Genesis through Judges—the remaining books are arranged in a significantly different order. Further complicating the definition of "the Bible" is that some Jewish religious texts, written at the end of the biblical period—the last few centuries before the Common Era and the first century or so of the Common Era—are not part of the Jewish Bible, although they were considered scripture by all Christians until the Reformation. These works, called "the Apocrypha" (meaning "hidden things," although there was never anything hidden about them), were dropped from Protestant Bibles beginning in the sixteenth century, but Roman Catholic and Orthodox Christian Bibles continue to include them. In this book, I usually use the term *Bible* in its most inclusive sense—any books that Jews and Christians have considered authoritative scripture.

The study of religion, and of religions, is one of many disciplines developed in the West since the Enlightenment. It shares with the study of history, for example, the helpful but also debatable notion that one can be objective: that one should strive to engage in that study without presuppositions, without an ax to grind, without a message to convey. An important corollary is that one does not need to be a believer to study religion. Christian scholars explore Hinduism, Jewish scholars explore Islam, and so forth. One recent example is *The Jewish Annotated New Testament*, in which Jewish scholars interpret the twenty-seven books of the New Testament.[3]

As a result both of scientific advances and of a more objective approach, beginning in the seventeenth century the Bible began to be viewed differently: as a book, or rather a collection of books, that could be read like any other. In 1670, the philosopher Spinoza stated that his goal was "to reexamine scripture with a fresh and free spirit."[4] With this freedom, he argued that Moses did not write the first five books of the Bible, the Torah or Pentateuch, contrary to long-held belief and official teaching. A few years later, a French Catholic priest, Richard Simon, reached similar conclusions in *A Critical History of the Old Testament*, a title whose words became the term for an important scholarly method for interpreting the Bible: historical criticism.[5]

Historical critics seek first of all to be critical, in the way that reviewers try to evaluate a book, a film, or a concert without prejudgment. In the study of the Bible, such an approach means understanding the Bible as a collection of works in many genres written by individuals in particular times and in particular places over many centuries. To interpret the Bible as a historical critic, then, is to look at it not as inspired and inerrant, as a revelation from on high, but on its own terms, as the words of David and Jeremiah, of Paul and John, and of other named and often unnamed authors. These authors did not think that they were writing sacred scripture as Jews and Christians would later come to view it.

Historical criticism developed among European Protestant scholars, especially in Germany, and became the dominant methodology for studying the Bible by the late nineteenth century. By the mid-twentieth century it had been embraced by many Jewish and Roman Catholic scholars, and it continues to be used by a majority of scholars alongside other interpretive strategies. Regardless of their religious background, these scholars—including me—form a broad consensus, agreeing both on the questions to be asked and on the answers to those questions.

Along with the shedding of presuppositions, another major factor affecting the interpretation of the Bible since the nineteenth century has been the discovery and decipherment of texts in many languages that are contemporaneous with the ancient biblical writings. Not only, it turns out, was the Bible not handed down by God from heaven in installments, but also in most respects it was not unique. Its ideas and values, its laws and institutions, its stories and myths, even its idioms resemble those of neighbors and rulers of the biblical writers, the ancient Babylonians, Egyptians, Canaanites, Greeks, Romans, and others. The biblical writers, after all, did not live in a vacuum.

In some circles, especially among religious conservatives, the historical-critical method has never been embraced, at least not fully. For such people, if Jesus attributed the book of Genesis to Moses, then Moses was its writer—if not its ultimate author. The Bible is, they believe, true in every sense. And although in the last few decades some scholars have declared that the historical-critical method has been superseded by other methodologies derived from the social sciences, literary criticism, and cultural criticism, no replacement has gained any consensus, and even those who write obituaries for historical criticism inevitably utilize it in their work.

What is not always admitted by both Jewish and Christian biblical scholars is that historical-critical investigation of their respective scriptures is fraught with tension. Most were, and continue to be, drawn to their specialization because of their religious background. Many were, and continue to be, active participants in their respective religious traditions. Many were, and also continue to be, ordained rabbis, priests, and ministers. That in itself is not surprising, but it has consequences. One is that many—if not most—scholars who are also believers suffer from what I would diagnose as a kind of intellectual schizophrenia. Here is an example: for the biblical writers, monotheism was neither obvious nor present from the beginning. However, monotheism, the belief in only one god, the biblical god, still informs the perspective of most biblical scholars. Although most of them do not think that the world was created in six days, that millions of Hebrews escaped from Egypt under Moses's leadership, or that Jesus was born in Bethlehem, and although most of them do not think that God is the author of the Bible, many of these scholars—along with most members of the religious communities to which they belong—continue to believe that God made at least one people, the ancient Israelites, his chosen people. Thus, they accept, at least implicitly, the authoritative status of the Bible as a kind of record of divine revelation, despite their professed objectivity.

For example, in his classic study *The Biblical Doctrine of Election*, the British biblical scholar H. H. Rowley, himself a Baptist, begins with a generalization with which few biblical scholars would disagree: "To the writers of the Old Testament Israel is the chosen people of God; to the writers of the New Testament the Church is the heir of the divine election."[6] Note how he speaks not of revelation from on high, but rather of what the biblical writers thought. Soon, however, this devolves into more dogmatic, faith-based assertions: "[God's] greatest purpose is to reveal Himself to men, and for that purpose Israel was chosen because Israel was most suited to it," and "the Church is . . . the heir of Israel in the very nature of its establishment." More recently, in his influential *Yet I Loved Jacob: Reclaiming the Biblical Concept of Election*, the American Jewish scholar Joel S. Kaminsky similarly accepts the biblical premise as valid: "Any universal horizon is only glimpsed through God's particularistic interaction with God's chosen people."[7] Both Rowley and Kaminsky, I would argue, are still inside their respective denominational boxes; they have not set aside their presuppositions. Their faith and their scholarship are implicitly at odds.

When I teach, I try to be careful not to promote my own views. My goal is not to get anyone to believe something or to stop believing something. I want to get students to think about what a text says, to consider what it meant when it was written, rather than what they presume it means. I also ask students to think about how the Bible is, or is not, relevant for today. At the end of one semester of teaching an introduction to the Hebrew Bible/Old Testament, a student asked me, "Are you Jewish or are you Christian?"—a question that to me at least indicated that I had succeeded in presenting the scriptures of ancient Israel and early Judaism objectively. In this sense, the study of the Bible is like the study of religion more generally. One does not need to be a Hindu to interpret the beliefs and practices of Hinduism, nor a Muslim or Jew or Christian to interpret Islam or Judaism or Christianity, respectively—although some believers in those traditions might disagree.

Complete objectivity, however, is an impossible ideal, for we are all influenced by our backgrounds. Here is my story. I was raised a Roman Catholic. In my childhood, we Catholics, attending parochial school, thought of ourselves as superior to our Protestant and Jewish neighbors who attended public school. We, after all, had the truth, by divine grace and divine choice. The others languished in partial knowledge or even in assured damnation.

The time was the 1950s, when the sense of being divinely chosen was a national, not just a denominational conviction. "Under God" was added to the Pledge of Allegiance to distinguish us Americans from our mortal enemies, the godless Communists of the Soviet Union. "Savior of the world, save Russia!" was a frequent prayer. I went to an all-boys Jesuit high school in New York City whose motto was *Deo et patriae* ("For God and the fatherland"). It had a very good Renaissance curriculum: four years of Latin, three of ancient Greek, two of German or French, plus English, theology, and some—not much—mathematics and science. It was very Catholic, with the smug intellectual superiority that Jesuits often display.

After high school, I joined those Jesuits, and over the course of the next ten years found my calling: the study of the Bible. I learned Hebrew and Aramaic, and with my superiors' blessing began graduate school in the Department of Near Eastern Languages and Literatures at Harvard University. I was swaddled in layers of chosenness and privilege, not a doubt in my mind.

All that changed, quickly, in May 1969. As a witness to and occasional participant in both the campus and the national opposition to what we call the Vietnam War (which the Vietnamese call the American War), I lost my faith in the institutions that had reinforced my sense of chosenness—the United States, the Roman Catholic Church, the Jesuits, and the university. At the same time, in my own intellectual development I was retracing the development of the historical-critical method. I came to realize that the Bible was not God's word but the words of men, mostly, and a few women who lived long ago, with assumptions often very different from ours. The Bible was not unique, and its claims of chosenness were also to be found in texts of its neighboring cultures. I stopped believing in the biblical god, or in any god. I left my swaddling clothes behind.

Let me digress briefly on the nature of the biblical god. In the Bible, God is in many respects a literary character, frequently described anthropomorphically. Like us—and like gods and goddesses in other ancient literatures—he can be angry, jealous, loving, vengeful, capricious, forgiving, and so on. He is only sometimes the more abstract god—the all-powerful, all-knowing, all-good supreme being—of philosophers and theologians. Still, this more abstract god is at least partially derived from the Bible, in whose various layers the more congenial and more sublime character of God can also be found. As I discuss the biblical god's choices of individuals and groups in the chapters that follow, I will focus mostly on how the Bible itself presents him, but I will also suggest that that presentation is not always consistent with how we would like God to be.

So, I write this book as a biblical scholar, fairly confident that I have brushed away the cobwebs of dogmatism and set aside my own presuppositions. As we work our way chronologically through representative biblical passages and their appropriations by later groups, we will find that chosenness is a self-designation for political and personal aggrandizement: just because individuals or groups assert that they have been chosen by God does not make it so, and just because it is in the Bible does not make it true. But I will further suggest that some biblical ideas and ideals might continue to inform our thinking and our actions today.

I also write this book in the perhaps naïve hope that just as many of us—scholars and students, believers and nonbelievers, Jews and Christians and others—have given up creationism, patriarchy, and homophobia (despite what the Bible says), so too (despite what the Bible says) might we abandon the tribalisms that lead one group to claim superiority over all others, tribalisms that are in effect unholy nationalisms that have had and continue to have lethal consequences. We should, I think, give up the myth of divine election, a myth that has caused so many walls to be built and wars to be waged between members of our human community rather than uniting it.

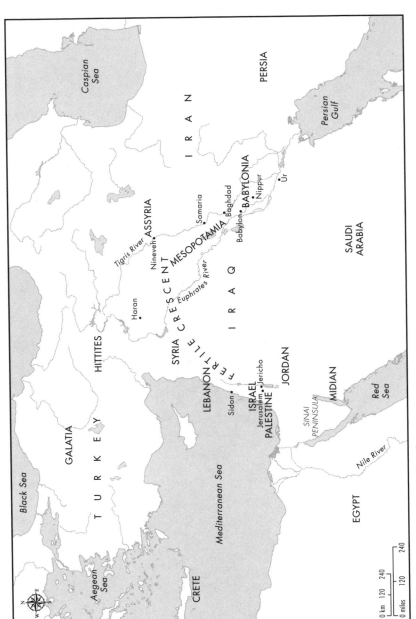

The Near East, with ancient and modern names.

2

ABRAHAM AND SONS

LIKE MOST ANCIENT NEAR EASTERN LITERATURE, the Hebrew Bible is the product of scribes who trained and practiced their profession in royal courts and temples. This literature thus has to do mostly with kings and gods, not ordinary people. But the first book of the Bible, Genesis, focuses mainly on ordinary individuals and especially on one family, the extended family of Abraham.

Abraham is the earliest person explicitly identified in the Bible as chosen by God, and his chosen status is transferred to his descendants from generation to generation.[1] His story in the book of Genesis echoes throughout the Bible and later writings over the centuries. But the story of Abraham is not a simple tale. Many books of the Bible were not written by single authors at single moments, but rather are the final product of scribal activity over many years and even centuries, combining, supplementing, reworking, and editing multiple sources. It is as if we had Malory's *Le Morte d'Arthur*, Tennyson's *Idylls of the King*, T. H. White's *The Once and Future King*, and Lerner and Loewe's *Camelot* all mixed together in a chronologically sequential collage about King Arthur and his entourage. As we examine the story of Abraham and his extended family over four generations, we need to keep in mind that different versions of that story are combined in Genesis.

Another analogy for the Bible's formation is the artificial mounds known as "tells" that dot the landscape of the Middle East.[2] These mounds are the result of successive periods of human activity, in which one town or city was built on top of another, for centuries and even for millennia. Each stratum or layer in a tell must be carefully excavated, distinguishing what is earlier and what is later. The stories of Abraham's extended family in Genesis are like those often-jumbled stratigraphic layers. Like ancient mounds, they require excavation.

So, although Genesis—and for that matter the first dozen or so books of the Bible—appears to present a chronologically sequential narrative, it is actually a layered text whose components come from different periods of the history of ancient Israel.[3] This means that as we examine the narratives, we will need to refer to persons and events that occurred later than those recounted in Genesis. Here is a brief synopsis of the history of ancient Israel as the biblical writers present it.

	TIMELINE*		
DATES	DOMINANT POWERS IN THE LEVANT	EVENTS	PERSONS
ca. 1550–1200 BCE	Egypt (south), Hittites (north)		
ca. 1250 BCE		Exodus from Egypt	Moses
ca. 1210		Entry of Israelites into land of Canaan	Joshua
ca. 1200–ca. 900 BCE	No dominant powers		
ca. 1150–1050		Period of the judges and rise of the Philistines	
ca. 1020		Establishment of the Israelite monarchy	Saul
ca. 1000–965		United Monarchy	David
ca. 968–928			Solomon
ca. 928		Split between the northern kingdom of Israel and the southern kingdom of Judah	
ca. 900–609 BCE	Assyria		
722		Assyrian conquest of northern kingdom of Israel	
701		Assyrian siege of Jerusalem	Isaiah; Hezekiah

DATES	DOMINANT POWERS IN THE LEVANT	EVENTS	PERSONS
609–539 BCE	**Babylonia**		
609		Babylonian defeat of Assyria	
597		Babylonian siege of Jerusalem	Jehoiachin; Jeremiah; Ezekiel
586		Babylonian destruction of Jerusalem	Zedekiah; Jeremiah; Ezekiel
539–332 BCE	**Persia**		
539		Persian capture of Babylon	Cyrus the Great
538		Cyrus allows Judean exiles to return	
520–515		Rebuilding of Jerusalem temple	
ca. 450		Missions of Ezra and Nehemiah	
332–63 BCE	**Greece**		
330		Alexander the Great defeats Persians	
63 BCE–330 CE	**Rome**		
ca. 30 CE		Crucifixion of Jesus of Nazareth	
ca. 50–60		Letters of Paul	
66–73		First Jewish Revolt against Rome	
70		Romans capture Jerusalem and destroy the temple	
ca. 70–80		Gospel of Mark	
ca. 80–90		Gospels of Matthew and Luke	
ca. 90–100		Gospel of John	
ca. 132–35		Second Jewish Revolt against Rome	

*Earlier dates are approximate and some are disputed.

For most of the periods covered in the next several chapters, the relatively small region known as the Levant—comprising modern Israel, Palestine, Jordan, Lebanon, and western Syria—was at various times under the control of much more powerful neighbors: Egypt to the south-southwest, the Hittites to the north, Assyria and Babylonia to the east in Mesopotamia, and Persia even farther east. Later still, the Greeks and then the Romans took over the region.

Biblical history takes place in this imperialistic context. For most of the second millennium BCE, the southern Levant was under Egyptian control. This is when the biblical writers date the events narrated in the first several books of the Bible: the generations of the patriarchs and matriarchs in the book of Genesis, the escape from slavery in Egypt and the journey to the Promised Land of Canaan in the books of Exodus through Deuteronomy, and the conquest and initial settlement of that land in the books of Joshua and Judges.

From about 1150 to 930 BCE, Egypt was relatively weak, and several smaller independent kingdoms—including ancient Israel and its neighbors, Ammon, Moab, Edom, Aram, and Tyre—formed in the Levant. During this period, ancient Israel comprised at first a loose confederation of tribes that traced their ancestry back to Jacob through his twelve sons, then a more organized chiefdom under Saul, and, finally, a monarchy under King David and his son Solomon in the tenth century BCE. That "united monarchy" split after Solomon's death into the southern kingdom of Judah, with its capital in Jerusalem, and the northern kingdom (somewhat confusingly also called Israel), which eventually had its capital in Samaria. These kingdoms gradually lost their autonomy as the northern Mesopotamian Assyrians took control of the entire Near East, including eventually even Egypt itself in 671 BCE. They captured the northern kingdom of Israel in 722 BCE and also laid siege to Jerusalem in 701, withdrawing when the king of Judah, Hezekiah, paid an enormous tribute.

In 609 BCE, an overextended and weakened Assyria was defeated by its southern neighbor, Babylonia, which took over the Assyrian empire. The kings of Judah alternated between subservience and rebellion, and when they rebelled, the Babylonians attacked.

Jerusalem was again besieged in 597 BCE; the king, Jehoiachin, surrendered and along with many members of his court was taken captive to Babylon. When Jehoiachin's successor, Zedekiah, also rebelled, the Babylonians under King Nebuchadrezzar captured and destroyed Jerusalem in 586. More Judeans—inhabitants of Judah— were deported. These deportations marked the beginning of the Babylonian exile, in which a significant proportion of Judeans were now dispersed, in a diaspora.

Babylonian rule of the Near East was brief, however. King Cyrus of Persia captured Babylon in 539 BCE and permitted Judean exiles there to return to Jerusalem. The newly returned Judeans rebuilt the temple that had been destroyed in 586 and enjoyed quasi-autonomy until the Persians in turn were defeated by the Greeks under Alexander the Great in 330 BCE. Alexander's successors continued to allow the Judeans relative independence, especially in religious matters, except for a brief period in the early second century BCE. By the early first century BCE, Rome had gained control of the Near East and, in response to unrest by Jews in Judea and elsewhere in the region, destroyed Jerusalem and its temple in 70 CE.

All of these events, and many more, made up the context in which the Jewish and Christian scriptures eventually known as the Bible were written, and thus they are essential for interpreting its layers. Now we return to Abraham.

Abraham's story as recounted in the book of Genesis begins with his father, Terah, moving from Ur in what is now southern Iraq, to Haran in southern Turkey, although he had intended to travel farther south to Canaan—territory we now know as Israel and Palestine. Terah brings with him his sons Nahor and Abram (as Abraham is called at first) and their wives as well as his grandson Lot, whose father, also named Haran, had died. Genesis also tells us that Abram's wife Sarai (later called Sarah) was infertile and that Terah died in Haran.[4] This is a story of migration: Genesis does not tell us why this family moved northwest to the center of the Fertile Crescent (the band of arable land that stretches north from the Persian Gulf, west across southeastern Turkey and northern Syria, and then south along the Mediterranean coast to Egypt). Such migrations were not unusual in antiquity and subsequently, especially by seminomadic pastoralists such as Abraham and his sons and grandsons. Some of these migrations were voluntary and some were forced, but in any case people were often on the move.

Migrations like Abraham's continue in the modern Middle East. On my first excavation in Israel, in 1968, a large group of seminomadic Bedouin living in tents were pasturing their sheep, goats, and camels on hillsides near our site. When the grass dried as summer advanced, they packed up to move, forming a large caravan of animals, women, and children on foot, with the sheikh comfortably leading in his Mercedes. Unhappily, migrations are more often compulsory. In this century, the most appalling example is Syria. The United Nations High Commissioner for Refugees estimates that of Syria's pre-2011 population of twenty-two million, over six million have been internally displaced and over five million are refugees in other countries.[5]

The stories of Abraham and his extended family are not historically verifiable. These people were at best extras on the set of world history, and nonbiblical records from palaces and temples show little interest in such minor characters. This obviously complicates the issue of when they might have lived. With no knowledge of Abraham—or of any other person in Genesis, for that matter—from possibly contemporaneous nonbiblical sources, we are left only with the Bible itself, whose chronology, especially in Genesis, is problematic at best. To give just one example, we are told that Abraham died at the age of 175, an impossible number. But his longevity was relatively modest compared to that of his ancestor Noah, who was 950 years old when he died, reportedly when Abraham was about 60. So, neither nonbiblical records nor biblical chronology enable us to determine when Abraham lived, and it is no wonder that modern scholars have dated him anywhere from 2500 to 1200 BCE, assuming he even existed.

Soon after the biblical writers introduce us to this family on the move, another character enters the story: Yahweh, later identified as the god of Israel. Readers of Genesis have met him earlier, beginning in the story of the Garden of Eden, but Abraham is apparently unfamiliar with him. Abruptly, Yahweh commands Abraham to leave his father's household and move on, promising him that he will make him into a great nation.[6] One biblical author has transformed an unremarkable family's story into one of divine call and promise. Abraham obeys the divine command and moves to Canaan.

The land of Canaan was not an empty land: it was the home of many groups, including "the Kenites, the Kenizzites, the Kadmonites, the Hittites, the Perizzites, the Rephaim, the Amorites, the Canaanites, the Girgashites, and the Jebusites" (Genesis 15:19–21). It was their land that was repeatedly promised to Abraham and subsequently to his son Isaac and to Isaac's son Jacob. If Abraham and his descendants were to possess it, then those others had to be dispossessed, for Yahweh apparently favored Abraham and his family more than he did those others.

Why did Yahweh favor Abraham? As often, the Bible is silent, giving no motive for the divine choice. In fact, from the very beginning of Genesis, Yahweh is disturbingly arbitrary. To give just two examples: Why did he put the forbidden tree of knowledge in the Garden of Eden if he did not want the man and woman to eat its fruit? Why did he prefer Abel's offering to that of Cain, Abel's older brother? The biblical writers give no answers to these questions and many others like them; their laconic style makes Yahweh appear not just mysterious, but even capricious. Much later, postbiblical writers invented answers, perhaps to make God seem more godlike. One elaboration of the terse biblical account of Abraham's early life is found in the nonbiblical book of *Jubilees*, written in the mid-second century BCE, long after Genesis was complete. It says that even when he was a boy, Abraham refused to worship idols, and that when he was sixty years old he set fire to the temple where those pagan deities were worshipped; that was why Terah and Abraham left Ur.[7] This is an example of what scholars call "rewritten Bible," in which later ancient authors take earlier biblical material and rework and expand it. In such retellings, as also repeatedly in the Qur'an, Abraham's monotheism is elaborated upon, becoming the reason for God's choosing him.[8]

The Bible, however, has none of this. The biblical writers here, as frequently elsewhere, leave gaps in their narrative. The final editors of biblical books were as comfortable with these gaps as they were with inconsistencies. Yahweh just told Abraham to go to Canaan, and Abraham obeyed. Once Abraham arrived there, Yahweh promised him that he would give that land to Abraham and to his seed, his offspring.[9]

But what offspring? As we were informed at the outset, Abraham had a big problem: he and his wife Sarah were childless. At Sarah's suggestion, Abraham took what anthropologists call a secondary wife, Sarah's Egyptian servant Hagar.[10] Like his contemporaries' families, Abraham's was not just patriarchal but also polygamous. Hagar immediately conceived and gave birth to Abraham's firstborn son, Ishmael. Clearly, then, Sarah was infertile, not Abraham. In biblical times infertility was always blamed on the woman: after all, the man produced seminal fluid, and sperm counts were not yet possible or even known about. As the firstborn son, Ishmael would have been his father's principal heir. The divine promise, the divine choice, would have transferred to him on his father's death.

Here we begin to excavate. Archaeological strata are never neat and straight: later material is not just superimposed on earlier, but often mixed into it, so what we encounter at the level of earlier material may in fact be later. The same applies to narratives about divine choice in Genesis. Although the narrative framework is sequential, the stories of how the expected, legal heir loses his status are from different authors and different periods. On one level, we are led to believe, it is because of Yahweh's plan, inscrutable as that may be. But in the stories themselves, human machinations often undercut the myth of divine choice. To put it differently, at times God and at other times individuals are responsible for the displacement of older sons by their younger brothers.

Ishmael is a case in point. Some years after Ishmael's birth, the biblical writers tell us, God appeared to Abraham again, making a legal agreement with him—a "covenant"—that bound both of them. For his part, God repeated his promise to give all the land of Canaan to Abraham and to his seed in perpetuity. In exchange, Abraham and all males in his household were to be circumcised, also in perpetuity. After an apparent digression, the circumcision of Abraham's household takes place, beginning with "Ishmael, his son" (Genesis 17:23). The plain sense of this episode is that God's covenantal promise to Abraham's descendants includes—in fact begins with—Ishmael.

But what about the digression? Coming from one of the latest layers in Genesis, added later into this earlier layer, it anticipates subsequent events: God speaks again to Abraham, and, prompting Abraham to laugh, promises that his ninety-year-old primary wife Sarah will also have a son. Moreover, God, apparently having changed his mind, says that the covenant will instead attach to Abraham's younger son, as yet not even born. Although according to biblical law the inheritance rights of the firstborn were inviolable and Ishmael should have been Abraham's principal heir to the divinely Promised Land, the digression anticipates Ishmael's loss of that inheritance.[11]

Genesis has two accounts, from different hands, of how this happened and how Ishmael and his mother were expelled from Abraham's household. In the first, Hagar fled from the household while she was still pregnant, because, we are told, this servant felt superior to Sarah, her barren mistress, and Sarah treated her harshly. In the wilderness, Hagar was comforted by a divine messenger, who gave her a variant of the promise of many descendants earlier given to Abraham and instructed her to return to live under Sarah's yoke.[12] So at first it seems that the soon-to-be born Ishmael will be Abraham's heir.

Finally, despite her advanced age, Sarah did have a son. As he had been instructed by God, Abraham named him Isaac (Hebrew *yitshaq*), from a word meaning "to laugh" (*tsahaq*).[13] Words having to do with laughter occur repeatedly in stories about Isaac, whose name means "[the deity] has laughed," that is, the patron god rejoices at the birth of this child. Then the troubles between Sarah and Hagar began anew, and we have a second account of Hagar and Ishmael's expulsion.

At a party to celebrate Isaac's having been weaned—probably at the age of two or three—Sarah saw Ishmael, then in his teens, "making her son Isaac laugh" (Genesis 21:9). Sarah's reaction was to tell Abraham to expel both Hagar and Ishmael—in effect to divorce Hagar—"for the son of this slave-woman will not inherit with my son Isaac" (Genesis 21:10). So one issue was clearly inheritance. But in this second account, something else is going on. That Ishmael was not simply amusing his much younger half-brother is hinted at by the apostle Paul, who speaks of Ishmael "persecuting" Isaac (Galatians 4:29). Later in Isaac's life, when he was residing in Gerar, a city in southern Canaan, he tried to pass off his wife as his sister, lest because of her beauty he be killed and she be taken. But one day the king of Gerar looked out of his window and saw Isaac "making his wife Rebekah laugh" (Genesis 26:8), and he immediately knew that she was not Isaac's sister because of what they were doing. Thus, Ishmael's making Isaac "laugh" has sexual innuendo, implying that he was sexually abusing Isaac.

As in other cultures, a recurring motif in Genesis is the derogatory depiction of other groups, especially the Israelites' neighbors, by attributing negative qualities to them or to their ancestors. Sometimes ancestors of such groups are described as engaging in sexual conduct that at least the biblical writers thought depraved. Thus, the Canaanites are descended from Noah's grandson Canaan, who was cursed because his father, Noah's son Ham, had "looked on his father's nakedness" (Genesis 9:22), probably hinting at incest either with his father or with his mother, Noah's wife. Similarly, the Ammonites and the Moabites, the Israelites' neighbors east of the Jordan River, are descended from Abraham's nephew Lot, who at his daughters' instigation, had sex with them after the destruction of Sodom, when they thought they were the only people in the world left alive.[14] Later, Reuben, Jacob's own firstborn son, lost his inheritance because he slept with Bilhah, one of his father's secondary wives.[15] In all of these cases, including the one hinting that Ishmael, the ancestor of Arabian tribes, sexually abused Isaac, the divine rejection of others is justified by describing their ancestors as sexual deviants in contrast to those who called themselves chosen.

So, once again, Hagar was expelled, and once again, she ended up in the wilderness with Ishmael, helpless and without water. Not wanting to see her son die of thirst, she placed him under a bush and sat down some distance away. And once again, she received divine comfort of a sort: once again God promised to make Ishmael into a great nation. One biblical layer, then, has God continue to protect and even to bless Ishmael, for although not chosen, he was Abraham's son. The promise of many offspring applies to him as well as to Isaac: Ishmael will go on to have twelve sons, like Isaac's chosen younger son Jacob. Moreover, Abraham will have another six sons by his third wife, Keturah, and Genesis lists almost lovingly the further offspring of this fertile and prolific patriarch: the offspring of Ishmael's twelve sons, Isaac's older son Esau's five sons (one by Ishmael's daughter) and their offspring, and Isaac's younger son Jacob's twelve sons (and twenty-one daughters) and their offspring.[16] The promise of possession of the land of Canaan, however, is given only to Abraham's second son Isaac, and then to Isaac's second son Jacob, also called Israel. Only the Israelites are truly chosen.

As the narrative has developed, what had apparently been just a family saga has become one of tribal rivalry, expressing the Isaac clan's sense of superiority over the Ishmael clan, a sense of superiority rationalized by self-proclaimed divine choice. But what some biblical writers describe as divine choice, others describe as the outcome of conflict between rival wives, with Abraham—and God—reluctantly acquiescing to Sarah's wishes and banishing Hagar and Ishmael. After the second account of Abraham's expulsion of Hagar and Ishmael, we encounter Ishmael only once more as a character in the Bible. The authors of Genesis conclude the story of Abraham by telling us that he made Isaac his primary heir, and that after his death his sons Ishmael and Isaac buried him.[17] This conclusion continues to maintain the dominant biblical view that Abraham's primary heir and the recipient of the covenant with God was his younger son Isaac, not his oldest son Ishmael. Similarly, as the family saga continues, Isaac's primary heir will be his younger son Jacob, not his firstborn son Esau.

The birth narrative of Esau and Jacob reintroduces the motif of a childless couple whose infertility miraculously ends. Like Sarah, Isaac's wife Rebekah was infertile. Other women in the same predicament include Jacob's second, favorite wife Rachel; the unnamed mother of the future Samson; Hannah, who became the prophet Samuel's mother; and, in the New Testament, Elizabeth, the eventual mother of John the Baptist. As with birth and infancy sagas of heroes in much ancient literature, the motif indicates that the offspring were born or survived against the odds because of divine intervention. God has a plan for them, and they are implicitly divinely chosen. So the birth narrative is a kind of overture to what follows.

Because Isaac and Rebekah had no children for twenty years after their marriage, Isaac prayed to Yahweh, and Yahweh answered his prayer: Rebekah became pregnant with twins.[18] Now another widespread motif recurs: that of rival brothers with the younger preferred. In Egyptian mythology, the god Seth kills his older brother Osiris, who then goes on to be ruler of the underworld, the lord of the west, where the sun shines while it is night on earth. In Roman legend, Romulus kills his twin brother Remus and goes on to found Rome. Sibling rivalry is also frequent in the Bible. Brothers, such as Aaron and Moses, vie with each other for power.[19] Sometimes the rivalry culminates in fratricide: Cain kills Abel; King David's son Absalom has his older half-brother, Amnon, killed. Later David's son and successor, Solomon, has his older half-brother, Adonijah, killed.[20] Sometimes the contending brothers are half-brothers from rival wives of the same father, like Ishmael and Isaac and the many sons of Jacob and of David. And sometimes they are twins, like Tamar and the patriarch Judah's sons (Perez and Zerah) and Rebekah and Isaac's sons (Esau and Jacob).[21]

During Rebekah's pregnancy, the twins' movement in her womb was uncomfortable, so she—not Isaac—sought divine guidance, which she received:

> *Two nations are in your belly,*
> *and two peoples will be divided from your abdomen.*
> *One people will be greater than the other,*
> *and the elder will serve the younger.*
> (Genesis 25:23)

This oracle is a snippet of poetry that immediately informs us of the gist of the story. It is not just about individuals, but about nations whose ancestors the brothers reportedly were, and about the conflicts between them. The "greater" nation is Israel, whose ancestor was Jacob, while the other is Edom, Israel's neighbor to the southeast, whose ancestor was Esau.

When the twins were born, Esau emerged first, followed by Jacob, whose hand was holding on to Esau's heel. A recurring narrative genre in ancient literature explains how persons and places got their names; such narratives are called *etiologies*. The core of an etiology is etymology—the meaning, or apparent meaning, of the name in question. Often these are folk etymologies, based on wordplay, and are not philologically accurate. The name Edom means "red"—like the layered sandstone of Petra, the "rose-red city half as old as time" in Edom, now southern Jordan. Stories about Esau highlight his redness. When Esau emerged from the birth canal, he was "all red, like a cloak of hair)"; the Hebrew word for *hair* is *se'ar* (Genesis 25:25). Another name for Edom in the Bible is Seir, perhaps because its once-forested hills looked from a distance as though they were covered with hair.[22] Later, when the twins had grown up, Esau, coming into the camp, saw Jacob cooking a pot of red lentils. Esau was so hungry that he sold Jacob his firstborn inheritance for the food.[23] So, not only was Esau red and hairy; he was also stupid: another put-down of a rival group's ancestor.

The narrator associates Jacob's name (in Hebrew, *ya'aqob*) with the word for "heel" (*'eqeb*), because he was grasping Esau's heel as he was born. This implied etymology, however, is not correct. Most ancient Near Eastern boys' names, given at birth, describe a deity or a deity's action. For example, the Hebrew name *Nathaniel*, means "God (*el*) has given [this child]"; that name can be abbreviated as Nathan. Names like *Jacob* are well attested in the ancient Near East; in them, the verb describing the deity's action means "to protect." So Jacob's name is a short form of a name that originally meant "[The deity] has protected [the family, by the birth of this child]," and it had nothing to do with "heel."

An alternate version of how Jacob got Esau's firstborn inheritance tells how Isaac, aged and blind, asked Esau to hunt and cook some game for him, after which Isaac would bless him—that is, in effect, formally give his older son title to his property. Our artful narrator engages in some wordplay here: in Hebrew, "firstborn inheritance" is *bekorah*, and "blessing" is *berakah*. Rebekah, overhearing her husband's words, tells Jacob, her favorite, to get two young goats, which she will cook for Jacob to bring to Isaac so that he will get the blessing instead of Esau.[24] To Jacob's objection that his father will recognize that he is not Esau because of his smooth skin, Rebekah says that she will take care of it and will suffer any consequences herself. Rebekah then cooks the kids, dresses Jacob in his brother's clothes—covering his arms and neck with the skins of the slaughtered animals—and gives him the meat and some bread. When Isaac asks Jacob who he is, Jacob lies: "I am Esau, your firstborn" (Genesis 27:19). Surprised that the game was caught and prepared so quickly, Isaac is suspicious and asks Jacob to come closer. Although he recognizes Jacob's voice, Isaac is convinced it really is Esau when he feels the apparently hairy arms, and gives Jacob the blessing, which includes a variation on the oracle given to Rebekah before the twins had been born:

> May peoples serve you,
> > and may nations bow down to you.
> May you be ruler over your brothers,
> > and may your mother's sons bow down to you.
> (Genesis 27:29)

Having gotten the blessing, Jacob quickly left. Soon after, the hapless Esau arrived, with the game he had caught and cooked. When Isaac realized what had happened, he was distraught, but once the blessing had been given it could not be withdrawn. Finally, in response to Esau's plea, Isaac gave him a blessing too:

> You will live by your sword,
> > but you will serve your brother.

> *But when you break free,*
>   *then you will tear off his yoke from your neck.*

(Genesis 27:40)

Both blessings announce that the relationship between the descendants of the twin brothers would be tempestuous. An alternate folk etymology for Jacob's name is given in this longer account of how Jacob usurped Esau's inheritance. When he discovered what had happened, Esau exclaimed: "Is he not rightly named Jacob? This is the second time he has cheated me," using the Hebrew word *wayya'qebeni* (Genesis 27:36). The verb "to cheat" is rare, and it is probably connected with the word for "heel," in the sense of stealthily coming up behind someone and grabbing his heel to trip him up, either literally or metaphorically. This is reflected in the prophet Hosea's description of Jacob's lifelong perfidy:

> *In the belly he grabbed his brother's heel/cheated him,*
>   *and in his prime he struggled with God;*
> *he struggled with an angel and he prevailed;*
>   *he wept, and asked for his favor.*
> (Hosea 12:3–4)

In these verses, Hosea is referring not only to the birth narrative of Esau and Jacob, but also to Jacob's nighttime wrestling match with a divine adversary (Genesis 32:22–32).

Enraged at the loss of his father's blessing and the inheritance that went with it, Esau planned to kill Jacob after Isaac died, so Jacob fled to northern Syria to live with Rebekah's family, again at Rebekah's suggestion. There he married his cousins Leah and Rachel and also their servants Zilpah and Bilhah as secondary wives. He eventually had twelve sons.

Jacob's story dominates the second half of the book of Genesis, which ends with his death. Jacob is the most fully developed human character in the book, more so than Adam, Eve, or Abraham. He is clever but flawed, loves one wife more than the other, and grieves the apparent loss of his favorite son Joseph. More space is devoted to him and his family than to anyone else in Genesis, because he is the primary ancestor of the nation of Israel, the name he was given by God after the nocturnal encounter.[25] From that point onward in the Bible, the patriarch Jacob will sometimes be referred to as Israel. His sons and their descendants are "the sons of Israel," that is, the Israelites.[26]

Although other biblical writers speak of Jacob as chosen by God, this is not directly stated in the Genesis narratives. The only possible indication of divine choice is the oracle given to Rebekah, but that is more prediction than decree. Rather, Jacob was chosen as Isaac's heir, and thus also as the heir of Yahweh's earlier promises to Abraham and to Isaac, not because of divine pronouncement but because of his own cleverness and especially because of his mother's scheming.

The various groups that in biblical times lived in the Levant were linked by closely related languages and culture, by intermarriage, and, as we now know, by their DNA. Ancient writers recognized this kinship and expressed it in genealogical narratives. So, in biblical tradition, the Ammonites and the Moabites in what is now modern Jordan—east of Israel—were descended from the sons of Abraham's nephew Lot by his two daughters. Similarly, tribes in Arabia were descended from Ishmael, Abraham's firstborn son by Hagar, and the Edomites—in southern Jordan—were descended from Esau, Jacob's twin. Jacob himself was the ancestor of the Israelites and his sons were identified as the ancestors of the tribes named for them. In the Bible, the genealogical narratives about these groups are one-sided, told from the Israelite perspective, so not surprisingly the others—the Ammonites, the Moabites, the Ishmaelites, and the Edomites—are depicted pejoratively. I suspect that if we had their equivalents to the book of Genesis, they would contain their own stories of how their national deities gave them superiority over the Israelites and each other.

The Israelites and the Edomites, whose ancestors were Jacob and Esau, had an especially close relationship; the Bible often refers to the two groups as "brothers."[27] Judging from sporadic biblical accounts, the interlocking history of Israel and Edom was one of occasional collaboration but also often one of frequent rivalry and conflict, like that of their supposed twin ancestors. In the late eleventh century BCE, one of the officials of Saul—the first king of Israel—was Doeg the Edomite, but Saul is also reported to have attacked Edom, and Saul's successor David is credited with subjugating all of Edom. During David's son Solomon's reign, however, the Edomites began to reassert their independence and thereafter we find reports of frequent interaction between the Edomites and both the northern kingdom of Israel and the southern kingdom of Judah, which had separated after Solomon's death. They were allies against their eastern neighbor Moab in the ninth century BCE, but also adversaries in the same period and subsequently. Hostilities between them explain occasional attacks on Edom in biblical literature from the first half of the first millennium BCE. Such antagonism was retrojected into the Edomites' refusal to let the Israelites pass through their territory during the period of the Israelites' wilderness wanderings after the Exodus from Egypt and, even earlier, to the stories of Esau and Jacob during the ancestral period in Genesis.

The antagonism between Edom and Israel reached a climax in 586 BCE, when the Babylonians destroyed Jerusalem, the capital city of the southern kingdom of Judah, and exiled many of its inhabitants to Babylon. It was the greatest disaster in Israelite history to that point, bringing to a traumatic end the ideas and institutions that had informed the nation's self-definition: that they were a people specially chosen by God with a land given them by divine grant, ruled over by the divinely chosen dynasty founded by King David, which had lasted some four centuries. According to several sources, the Edomites joined with the Babylonians in their destruction of Jerusalem and themselves had burned the temple that King Solomon had built there in the tenth century.

Biblical literature of the sixth century BCE has repeated diatribes against the Edomites. Psalm 137, which begins so poignantly—"By the rivers of Babylon, there we sat, and we wept when we remembered Zion"—ends with a violent curse:

> Remember, Yahweh, the day of Jerusalem against the sons of Edom,
>   who said: "Tear it down! Tear it down to its foundation!"
> O daughter of Babylon, you destroyer:
> Blessed is he who pays you back
>   what you have done to us!
> Blessed is he who seizes your babies,
>   and smashes them on the rock!

Vindictive passages such as this, blaming the Babylonians and the Edomites for Jerusalem's destruction, ignore an important alternate view presented in other parts of the Bible. Vindictiveness often co-exists with awareness of guilt: according to many biblical writers, the events of the early sixth century BCE were ultimately caused by Yahweh, who was punishing his people for their failure to worship only him. In this theological understanding, Nebuchadrezzar, the king of Babylon, was Yahweh's "servant," acting as his agent and at his command.[28] Why then, we might ask, should Judah's enemies be blamed for what they had done, when they were simply tools in the divine hand?

But vindictiveness is also frequent. For example, in the latest parts of the book of Isaiah, written in the sixth or fifth century BCE, anonymous prophets proclaim divine vengeance on Edom in gory detail. One passage, the inspiration for the opening stanza of Julia Ward Howe's "The Battle Hymn of the Republic," announces the divine defeat of Edom and its capital Bozrah in an imagined dialogue between the prophet and Yahweh:

> "Who is this coming from Edom,
>   in crimson clothing from Bozrah? . . ."
> "It is I, announcing victory,
>   mighty in deliverance."

"Why are your garments red,
  and your clothing like one treading in a wine press? . . ."
"I trod them in my anger,
  and I trampled them in my rage.
Their juice spattered on my clothing,
  and all my garments were stained."
(Isaiah 63:1–3; see also 34:5–8)

A violent god is punishing the alleged enemies of his chosen people; Yahweh has apparently forgotten that he himself was ultimately responsible for Jerusalem's destruction.

Even more troubling is a passage in the short book of Malachi. Written not much later than that in Isaiah quoted above, it calls Edom "the people whom Yahweh cursed forever," and explains why: even though Esau and Jacob are brothers, Yahweh says, "I love Jacob, and I hate Esau" (Malachi 1:2–3). The authors of Genesis never said that God loved only Jacob and hated Esau, but here a perhaps understandable post-traumatic nationalistic fervor claims just that.

But we must further ask: what sort of a deity shows such favoritism? In the New Testament, the apostle Paul squarely faces the conundrum of apparently arbitrary divine choice in his letter to the Romans. He begins by summarizing the oracle to Rebekah, quotes Malachi 1:3, and directly addresses the issue of God's favoritism:

What then should we say? Is there injustice on God's part? Of course not! For he says to Moses, "I will have mercy on whomever I have mercy, and I will show compassion to whomever I show compassion."[29] So it depends not upon a person's will or effort, but upon God being merciful. (Romans 9:14–16)

Clearly Paul is troubled by the shocking statement in Malachi. His emphatic denial that God can be unjust betrays his discomfort, but his answer is hardly satisfactory. In the end, God is arbitrary, according even to Paul, as the repeated hardening of Pharaoh's heart in the book of Exodus shows, and to which Paul turns next. For Paul, the answer to this theological dilemma lies in human ignorance: "Who are you, O human being, to answer back to God?" (Romans 9:20). But this begs the question: is God unjust? Apparently so, arbitrarily loving Jacob and hating Esau and hardening Pharaoh's heart so that an insecure deity might show his power to the whole world.

Contemporary scholars are not always as honest as Paul. In his book on the divine choice of Israel, Joel Kaminsky completely ignores the words "I have hated Esau" in Malachi 1:3; the verse is not even listed in his index of ancient sources.[30] Similarly, in his highly regarded commentary on Paul's letter to the Romans, Joseph A. Fitzmyer describes God's hating Esau as "an ancient Near Eastern hyperbole," and paraphrases "hated" as "loved less."[31] Both, I think, recoil from the notion of a capricious and unjust deity, despite what some biblical writers clearly say. But not all biblical writers. Surely this is not how God should act, as Abraham reportedly recognized when he challenged Yahweh about the divine plan to destroy innocent citizens of Sodom along with the guilty ones: "Should not the judge of all the earth do what is right?" (Genesis 18:25). So, the choice of Jacob over Esau—and ultimately of Israel over all its neighbors—if divine at all, is indefensible. Simply to call it mysterious is an abdication of reason.

Written long after the events they purportedly describe, the Genesis narratives are a projection back into ancestral times of the ongoing history between the Israelites and their neighbors. Other biblical writers, writing from a similarly partisan perspective, framed this in the language of divine choice, using horribly violent language to justify their nationalism. But that choice, as we have seen, is not necessarily divine. In Genesis, it is also presented as a family drama, with rival wives and brothers repeatedly scheming to gain status for themselves and their offspring. The authors of narratives about them drew not on divine decree, but on stock literary genres and motifs, in order to privilege Abraham, Isaac, and Jacob and their descendants over Ishmael and Esau and their descendants. This, then, is literature—not revelation.

In other words, some writers of Genesis imply, God himself chose neither Isaac nor Jacob. Ishmael was also Abraham's son, and the last we see of him is his joining his younger brother in burying their father, just as Esau and Jacob together would later bury their father, Isaac, in the same family tomb. The same filial piety will be repeated in Jacob's burial, when, despite their many conflicts and tensions, all twelve of his sons accompany his mummified body from Egypt to Canaan and bury him alongside Abraham and Sarah, Isaac and Rebekah, and Leah in the cave at Machpelah, now a contested Jewish and Muslim shrine in Hebron in the West Bank. All of this may be narrative boilerplate: when telling the story of a revered ancestor, it was appropriate to conclude with his burial by all of his sons. Still, in these brief burial notices, no son—not Ishmael, not Esau, not Reuben or Simeon or Levi—is absent or estranged. But these unremarkable, conventional stories have been overlaid with more gripping ones of sibling rivalry, which themselves personalize centuries of tribal and national conflicts, and have been elevated to the myth that God chose Israel—and only Israel. That myth became canonical, permeating biblical literature and subsequent history with tragic consequences.

3

HIS NAME IS JEALOUS

(Exodus 34:14)

BY THE END OF THE BOOK OF GENESIS, Jacob and his extended family—some seventy persons in all, we are told—had immigrated to Egypt because of a famine in Canaan. For several generations they prospered there. But eventually the Egyptian ruler, the pharaoh, alarmed by their rapid growth, decided to exterminate them. This is the first account of genocide against the Jewish people.

The story of the Exodus from Egypt that follows takes up the rest of the Torah, or Pentateuch, the Bible's first five books. The human hero of the Exodus is Moses, Jacob's great-great-grandson. The beginning of the book of Exodus, the Torah's second book, narrates Moses's early life. His death occurs at the end of Deuteronomy, the Torah's fifth and last book, as the Israelites have reached the Jordan River, the eastern boundary of the Promised Land. In a familiar pattern, Moses was also the younger brother of Aaron, who was both Moses's rival and subordinate, as well as the first high priest.[1]

The Exodus is the paradigmatic event in the Bible, an archetype for the description and interpretation of subsequent events in both the Jewish and the Christian scriptures. It is a story of liberation and of a journey toward home. Above all it is the story of how Yahweh, the god of Israel, intervened on behalf of his chosen people to return them to the Promised Land. Under Moses's leadership the Israelites escaped from Egypt, after Yahweh had forced the Egyptians to let them go by unleashing a series of increasingly deadly plagues that afflicted the Egyptians but not the Israelites. As the Israelites fled, Yahweh parted the waters of the Red Sea for them, then caused their pursuers—"Pharaoh and all his army" (Exodus 14:17)—to drown as the waters returned.[2]

On one level the story of the Exodus is clearly mythical: Yahweh is one of the main protagonists. But could it also be historical? Egyptian sources make no mention of Moses, nor of a swift series of plagues culminating with the death of firstborn, nor of a massive defeat of the Egyptian army. Moreover, biblical sources are tantalizingly vague: as is also the case for the pharaohs mentioned in the book of Genesis, neither of the two pharaohs mentioned in the book of Exodus is named; were their names given, we would at least know when the biblical writers thought the events in which they play a role took place.[3] Finally, the Bible simply exaggerates: how many Israelites left Egypt? According to one source, some six hundred thousand men, not counting women, children, fellow travelers, and livestock—an impossible number demographically and one without any supporting archaeological data.[4] Still, beneath all the layers of exaggeration accumulating over the centuries is likely an authentic historical kernel: a group of Hebrews in Egypt successfully escaped from slave labor, most likely in the mid-thirteenth century BCE. The human leader of that escape was Moses, who, like Aaron, Phinehas, and other characters in the narrative, has an Egyptian name. Ultimately, however, the escapees attributed their deliverance to divine intervention on their behalf.

This story of divine deliverance has inspired believers for thousands of years. It has become the basis for many positive theologies. In freeing Jacob's descendants from slavery in Egypt, Yahweh showed himself to be a god deeply and passionately involved in human history, one with what twentieth-century liberation theologians called "a preferential option for the poor." The divine action in the Exodus, they argued, is a model for how humans are to act toward the marginalized. As an underlying principle of biblical ethics, imitation of God would appear to be unassailable: he is the freer of slaves, the father of orphans, the defender of widows, and the protector of immigrants, and humans should follow his example.[5]

But the paradigmatic event of the Exodus also has a dark side. True, Yahweh does free the Israelite slaves, but there were other slaves in Egypt, not belonging to the chosen people. The last of the plagues, the climax of a crescendo of one-sided divine violence, is the killing of the firstborn in Egypt. As he had earlier threatened, Yahweh kills Pharaoh's firstborn son, a kind of quid pro quo for Pharaoh's treatment of Israel, Yahweh's firstborn.[6] But what about all the other firstborn in Egypt, who also die: "The firstborn of the slave girl who is at the mill, . . . the firstborn of the captive in the dungeon, and all the first-born of the cattle" (Exodus 11:5; 12:29)? Yahweh's mercy and love, it would seem, extend only to his chosen ones, not to other slaves and not to animals, at least not in Egypt.

Furthermore, were all those plagues—the frogs, the flies, the boils, the locusts, and so on—really necessary? According to the narra-tive, Pharaoh would have released the Israelites sooner, but Yahweh repeatedly "hardened Pharaoh's heart."[7] So troubling is this notion that some biblical sources put it differently: Pharaoh's heart was hard-ened,[8] or he hardened his own heart.[9] Such theologically fussy rewrit-ing attempts unsuccessfully to soften the original, in which Yahweh himself was responsible for the succession of plagues by making Pha-raoh unwilling to let the Israelites go. Why would he do this? The text repeatedly tells us: so that the Egyptians would recognize that there is no god like him.[10] At this stage, at least, Yahweh was not a monothe-ist himself. In the announcement of the terrible final plague, he says:

> I will pass through the land of Egypt tonight, and I will strike every firstborn in the land of Egypt, humans and animals. And on all the gods of Egypt I will execute judgments. I am Yahweh! (Exodus 12:12)

An apparently insecure god needs to show that he is the most pow-erful deity, even more powerful than the many deities of powerful Egypt; to achieve this goal all Egypt must suffer. And the Israelites at least get the point: after the escape at the sea, they proclaim, "Who is like you, Yahweh, among the gods?" (Exodus 15:11). In the mythical level of the Exodus story, the god of Israel scarcely resembles the only God of later Jewish, Christian, and Muslim believers and thinkers, and is hardly a model for human conduct.

Where did Yahweh come from? After their escape from Egypt, the Israelites traveled to Mount Sinai in the land of Midian, likely somewhere in what is now southern Jordan and northwestern Saudi Arabia, just east of the eastern arm of the Red Sea.[11] Moses had been there before. As a young man he had killed an Egyptian who was beating one of Moses's fellow Israelites, and fled Egyptian jurisdiction to the east, settling in Midian, where he married Zipporah, the daughter of the priest of Midian.[12] One day, while tending his father-in-law's flock, he came to the mountain of God, Horeb (as Mount Sinai is sometimes called), where God appeared to him in a burning bush. At the beginning of what turns out to be an extended conversation, God identifies himself to Moses as the god of the Israelites' ancestors, Abraham, Isaac, and Jacob. When Moses politely asks what his name is, God is somewhat evasive, first replying "I am who I am" (Exodus 3:14), implying that his name was none of Moses's business, and only later disclosing his personal name, Yahweh; in the Bible as in other literatures, divine beings were often reluctant to reveal their names.[13] So, it seems, Moses did not know the deity who appeared to him.

The earliest nonbiblical text that mentions the deity Yahweh specifically is from the ninth century BCE, when he was already established as Israel's national god. But there is more: Egyptian texts often mention the Shasu, a nomadic group of tribes in the southern Levant. Two texts, from the fourteenth and thirteenth centuries BCE, locate some of the Shasu more precisely: in the land of Seir and in the land of Yahweh.[14] Seir is another name for Edom, in southern Jordan, and so here "Yahweh" may also be a place name, likely derived from the name of the local deity. Early biblical poetry connects Yahweh with this region:

> Yahweh, when you set out from Seir,
>   when you marched from the pastureland of Edom,
> the earth quaked,

> and the heavens dripped,
>   and the clouds dripped water;
> the mountains shuddered
>   before Yahweh, the one of Sinai,
>   before Yahweh, the god of Israel.
>   (Judges 5:4–5)

Sinai, in Edom, is thus Yahweh's original home:

> Yahweh came from Sinai,
>   and dawned from Seir upon us;
>   he shone forth from Mount Paran:
> with him were myriads of holy ones.
>   (Deuteronomy 33:2)[15]

Piecing together these fragments of biblical and nonbiblical sources, we can conclude that Yahweh was originally a tribal deity of Midian, whose priest was Moses's father-in-law. As in many interfaith marriages, Moses adopted his wife's family's religion, and they worshipped together.[16]

Even the latest biblical sources, written when monotheism had developed, recognize that something new occurred at Sinai. In a variant of Yahweh's conversation with Moses at the burning bush, he tells him: "I am Yahweh. I appeared to Abraham, to Isaac, and to Jacob as El Shadday, but by my name Yahweh I was not known to them" (Exodus 6:2–3). Immediately we must ask, then whom did the Israelites' ancestors worship? According to this late source, not Yahweh, even though in some earlier sources in Genesis they often did know and worship him by that name.[17] Rather, the text tells us, preserving an ancient and credible tradition, they worshipped El Shadday. El, whose name simply means "god," was the head of the Canaanite pantheon. Shadday was one of his many epithets; its meaning is disputed, and possibilities include "the one of the mountain" and "the one of the wilderness." Apparently Jacob's descendants did not worship Yahweh in Egypt either, until Moses converted them to his father-in-law's belief.[18] In other words, they were not yet monotheists. The worship of El by the Israelites' ancestors is one of the earliest layers of biblical religion, preserved in Israel's very name and despite repeated insistence by most biblical writers that Yahweh was the only god to be worshipped, and eventually the only god.[19]

During their lengthy conversation at the burning bush, God promised Moses that he and the soon-to-be-rescued Israelites would worship him on the same mountain where he was now standing. Then, following divine instructions, Moses went back to Egypt, where he introduced his brother Aaron to the worship of this new deity, and together they persuaded the Israelites to believe in him as well. A month after the Exodus, they arrived at Sinai and camped at its base. There Yahweh instructed Moses to proclaim to them:

> You saw what I did to Egypt and how I lifted you on vultures' wings and brought you to me. And now, if you will truly listen to my voice, and keep my covenant, then you will become for me a possession more treasured than all peoples, for all the earth is mine, and you will become for me a kingdom of priests and a holy nation. (Exodus 19:4–6)

Here, in a kind of litany of terms for chosenness, Yahweh describes how he thinks of the Israelites. First, they are his "treasured possession." The Hebrew word used here, *segullah*, is relatively rare in the Bible. Usually it describes the Israelites' relationship to God: they are his personal property.[20] An early biblical poem expands on this aspect of the relationship between Yahweh and Israel:

> *When the Most High allotted to each nation its property,*
> *   when he divided up human beings,*
> *he set the boundaries of peoples*
> *   according to the number of gods;*
> *but Yahweh's own portion was his people,*
> *   Jacob was his allotted share.*
> (Deuteronomy 32:8)[21]

The text describes a mythological scene, when the Most High god (probably, although not necessarily, Yahweh), divides up humankind into national groups, making as many nations as there are gods and goddesses in his pantheon. Each deity becomes the patron of one group, but Yahweh saves Israel for himself. The Israelites' special status, then, is based on their being Yahweh's own people, who have a unique relationship with him.

That relationship is further described in Exodus 19: the Israelites are "a kingdom of priests and a holy nation."[22] Because of their closeness to Yahweh, the Israelites are holy, like priests. There may even be a hint here that as such they are the mediators between Yahweh and the rest of humanity, a motif that will be developed in later biblical literature.[23]

But the Israelites' special status entailed responsibilities, which Yahweh also mentions, first in summary: the Israelites must obey him, that is, they must keep his "covenant," a term borrowed from the practice of law. A covenant or testament (so called because it was witnessed) was a formal, binding agreement between two parties; the Bible uses the word translated as "covenant" for what we know as treaties, property transactions (including slavery), and marriage contracts. The use of this secular legal terminology for the relationship between Yahweh and the Israelites is thus metaphorical: collectively, the Israelites are, as it were, Yahweh's treaty vassal, his property, and his wife. The covenant at Sinai differs from the earlier ones made with Abraham, Isaac, and Jacob, because it is conditional: the Israelites' status as Yahweh's chosen people is dependent on their obedience to him. What Yahweh wants is detailed in the Decalogue, the Ten Commandments, which is in effect the text of the contract or covenant. It begins:

> I am Yahweh, your god, who brought you out from the land of Egypt, from the house of slaves. You should have no other gods besides me. (Exodus 20:2–3; Deuteronomy 5:6–7)

Here Yahweh summarizes what he had done for the Israelites, and then announces what he requires in return: they are to worship only him. This is not monotheism in the strict sense, denying that other gods exist; that will be articulated only late in the biblical period. Rather, among the many gods who might be worshipped, the Israelites may worship only one. This is odd, for all other ancient (and some modern) religions worshipped many gods simultaneously. Why does Yahweh insist on such exclusive worship? The Decalogue itself tells us: "For I, Yahweh, your god, am a jealous god" (Exodus 20:5; Deuteronomy 5:9).

The Hebrew word translated as "jealous" and other etymologically related words encompass a semantic field having to do with passion, envy, and zeal, as well as jealousy, as of the sexual jealousy of a husband over another man's attention to his wife.[24] Because one of the legal analogues for the "covenant" between God and the Israelites is the marriage contract, Yahweh forbids the Israelites to worship other, rival gods, just as an ancient Israelite husband would brook no rivals for his wife's sexual favors. As the prophets Hosea and Ezekiel develop in extended allegories, Yahweh is a jealous husband, and his jealousy has severe ramifications in allegorical spousal abuse.[25]

On one level, we have a fiercely jealous mountain god revealing himself to Moses and to the Israelites and wreaking havoc on the Egyptians and others he had not chosen. Worried that his new adherents would revert to their earlier worship of other gods, he insisted that they worship only him. But the texts were written by human authors, so we also need to ask why, unlike their contemporaries, they felt the need to restrict their worship to a single deity. It may have had something to do with who they were: a tribe, landless for a time at least, who found some security, for a time at least, with another tribe in the rugged territory of Midian, whose deity they adopted as their own.[26] This small tribe of refugees may not have had the resources to worship more than one deity, and they made a virtue out of necessity.

Moses had not only married into a Midianite family, but he also adopted their local tribal deity and their legal system.[27] So Yahweh became the god of Israel, and insistence on worshipping him and only him occurs in the earliest layers of biblical tradition. This same exclusivity later applies to those who would join the people of Israel: they must choose to worship only him rather than the gods of Mesopotamia, Egypt, and Canaan as they had done before.[28]

The book of Deuteronomy, which has the form of several farewell addresses given by Moses shortly before his death, is more explicit and more insistent that the Israelites are uniquely chosen than any other part of the Bible. Here is a representative passage:

> It was not because you were the most numerous of all peoples that Yahweh embraced you and chose you; in fact, you are the smallest of all peoples! Rather, it was because of Yahweh's love for you. (Deuteronomy 7:7–8)

Deuteronomy also repeatedly commands the Israelites to worship Yahweh exclusively. "Hear, O Israel: Yahweh is our god, Yahweh alone" (Deuteronomy 6:4), Moses instructs them, in words that will become the opening of a daily prayer for Jews, the Shema. So insistent is Yahweh that only he is to be worshipped that he commands the Israelites to exterminate those who worship other gods when the Israelites take possession of their lands, to put them under "the ban."[29] That is a technical term (the Hebrew word is *herem*, related to the English word *harem*) meaning something set apart—in the Bible, set apart for God. It involves total extermination, often including livestock: "You should not let anything that breathes live" (Deuteronomy 20:16). Just as Yahweh's inferiority complex led him to wreak havoc among the Egyptians, now it is catastrophic for other groups as well: he cannot tolerate worshippers of other gods.

Following the divine command, that is exactly what the Israelites did, at least according to the book of Joshua, after they entered Canaan under Moses's successor Joshua's leadership. At Jericho, "they put under the ban everything in the city, men and women, young and old, oxen and sheep and donkeys, with the edge of the sword" (Joshua 6:21), and they did the same with all the other cities of Canaan.[30] Equally shocking is the divine role in this. As he had done to Pharaoh during the plagues in Egypt, Yahweh hardened the hearts of those living in the Promised Land:

It was Yahweh's doing to harden their hearts, to meet Israel in battle, so that they might be put under the ban, without there being any mercy for them but rather to destroy them, as Yahweh had commanded Moses. (Joshua 11:20)

Like most other aspects of ancient Israelite religion, mass slaughter of conquered populations was not unique to the Israelites. In one of very few texts from ancient Moab—Israel's neighbor east of the Dead Sea—Mesha, a king of Moab in the mid-ninth century BCE, relates how the principal deity of Moab, Chemosh, had commanded him, using the same technical term:

"Go, take Nebo from Israel!" So I went by night and attacked it from daybreak until noon, and I took it. And I killed everyone in it, seven thousand men, boys, women, girls, and slave women. For I had put it under the ban for Ashtar-Chemosh.

So, Yahweh was not just jealous of other gods but was like them, too, despite assertions of his uniqueness.

As with the Exodus, there is no compelling nonbiblical evidence, either textual or archaeological, for a massive conquest of the land of Canaan with accompanying genocide, and the Bible itself contains contradictory data. The book of Judges, which immediately follows the book of Joshua, opens with a kind of prose catalogue of most of the Israelite tribes, reporting how they did not in fact wipe out the inhabitants of the land.[31] So, for example, "Ephraim did not drive out the Canaanites who lived in Gezer, but the Canaanites lived among them in Gezer" (Judges 1:29). For these reasons, many scholars have suggested that the "ban" was only a theory, a kind of hyperbolic ideal to convey the importance of exclusive worship of Yahweh. But as in the Exodus narrative, historical or not, we find in the Joshua narrative, historical or not, the same depiction of an obsessively jealous and bloodthirsty god. And again, like it or not, this is the biblical god, who has no love or even mercy for those he has not chosen, including their animals.

This obsessive divine jealousy also applies to those of his chosen people who break the command to worship only him:

> If you hear it said of one of the cities that Yahweh, your god, is giving you to dwell in, that worthless men have gone out from among you, and have led astray the inhabitants of their city, saying: "Let us go and serve other gods," whom you have not known, . . . then you should strike the inhabitants of that city with the edge of the sword, put it under the ban, all that is in it, and its cattle." (Deuteronomy 13:12–13, 15)

The same punishment is to be meted out even to members of one's own family—brothers, children, wife.[32]

As he is described in the pages of the Bible, God is not just capricious in his choice of one individual or group over another, but he is also violent toward those who worship other gods, even when they belong to his chosen people. Collectively they were, metaphorically, married only to him: if they strayed, he would severely punish them. The prophet Ezekiel vividly describes Yahweh's rage for his personified covenant partner, who had been unfaithful to him by worshipping other gods:

> I will gather all your lovers in whom you took such delight, . . . and I will uncover your nakedness to them. . . . They will strip off your clothes and take your beautiful ornaments and leave you naked and nude. They will bring up a mob against you, who will stone you and hack you with their swords. . . . So I will put a stop to your promiscuity. (Ezekiel 16:37–41)

One of the most appalling corollaries of Yahweh's exclusive choice of the Israelites is what it means for those not chosen. A few biblical writers reject this understanding of an arbitrary, all-too-human deity. The book of Jonah, for example, insists on Yahweh's concern for non-Israelites and even for their animals; speaking of the capital of Assyria, Israel's enemy from the ninth to the seventh centuries BCE,

Yahweh says, "Should I not have pity on Nineveh, that great city, in which there are more than a hundred twenty thousand people . . . and many animals?" (Jonah 4:11).

Still, the dominant biblical view is that Yahweh was selective in whom he chose. The others, not chosen, were despised not only by the writers, but also, according to them, by Yahweh: he freed some slaves, became a father to some orphans, defended some widows, and protected some immigrants, but made others slaves, orphans, widows, and refugees. We can reject the writers' understanding of Yahweh as all too human, and conclude that they are projecting onto him their own prejudices and practices, rationalizing their tribalism by cloaking it in the myth of divine choice and divine command. But if we do this, then the Bible's authority is irrevocably undermined: it is not a revelation from God about God, but simply a human creation.

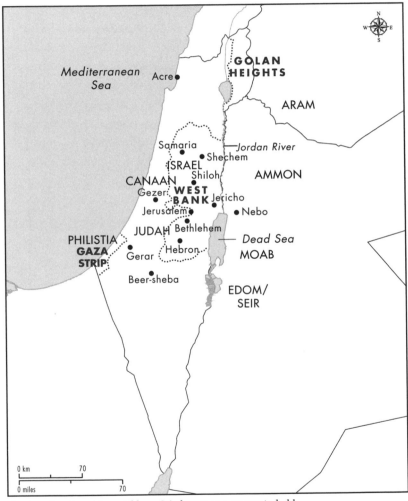

Ancient Israel and its neighbors. Modern terms appear in bold.

4

DIVINELY CHOSEN KINGS AND KINGDOMS

ALTHOUGH THE ISRAELITES evidently chose the Midianite deity Yahweh as their tribal god, for some biblical writers the choice is reversed: Yahweh chose the Israelites, and only them, as a special possession, an assertion found in every layer of biblical tradition. At first, the texts tell us, Yahweh chose all those descended from Jacob, "the sons of Israel." But over time, we also find in the Bible degrees of chosenness among the Israelites: some groups, and especially some individuals, turn out to be more chosen than others.

In biblical narrative, the Israelites' escape from Egypt under Moses and their entry into the Promised Land under Joshua was followed by two centuries of instability. This was caused in part by their decentralized political structure: twelve loosely affiliated tribes, with at best a volunteer militia, who were often at the mercy of better organized states on their borders. For the biblical writers, however, this was not the inevitable result of the strong defeating the weak; rather, it was divinely imposed punishment for the Israelites' failures to worship only Yahweh. As the situation deteriorated, the Israelites' worst enemy became the Philistines, also recently arrived in Canaan, from the Aegean. With a centralized collective government and superior military technology, the Philistines swiftly expanded to the north and east from their original settlement on the southeastern Mediterranean coast. By the late eleventh century BCE, their strength and geographical reach threatened Israel's very existence.

The Israelites' response to this crisis was to become a monarchy, with a strong central government and a standing army. Although some conservatives at the time reportedly saw this as a rejection of Yahweh's kingship, realpolitik was more influential than theology: pragmatic voices recognized the benefit in having a king, like other nations, "to go out before us and to fight our battles" (1 Samuel 8:20).[1] The promonarchy faction even described this as divine initiative, with the first king, Saul, explicitly chosen by Yahweh, who had reportedly instructed the old prophet Samuel: "You should anoint him as leader over my people Israel, for he will save my people from the power of the Philistines" (1 Samuel 9:16).

The idea that a ruler, and not just a people, was divinely chosen is commonplace in royal propaganda throughout history. In an inscription commemorating the rebuilding of the city wall of Sippar, south of modern Baghdad, Iraq, the eighteenth-century BCE Babylonian king Hammurapi declared:

> [The sun god] Shamash, the great lord of heaven and earth, the king of the gods, with a content face joyfully looked at me, Hammurapi, the prince, his favorite, granted me an eternal kingship, a reign of long days, set firm for me the foundations of the land that he had given to me to rule.[2]

Thus, Hammurapi's rule, like the institution of kingship itself, was "lowered from heaven," as a recurring formula puts it.[3]

In other texts from his reign, Hammurapi makes the same assertion: the gods had given him rule over Babylon because they had specially chosen him. The most elaborate version of this claim of divine choice is found in the prologue to his famous Code, where he alludes to the myth recounted in the Babylonian creation epic, Enuma Elish. Reflecting the growing dominance of Babylon in the region, Enuma Elish recounts how kingship over the gods passed from Enlil, the chief deity of Nippur in southern Mesopotamia, to Marduk, the chief god of Babylon. Marduk then proceeded to defeat the primeval sea monster, after which he established the cosmos and presided over the creation of humans. Hammurapi links his assumption of kingship over Babylon to Marduk's assumption of kingship over the gods and humans, and identifies himself as the divinely chosen shepherd of his subjects.[4]

Hammurapi was not the only ancient Near Eastern king who claimed to have been divinely chosen. To give just two examples of many, Nebuchadrezzar, king of Babylon in the late seventh and early sixth centuries BCE, identified himself as "the loyal shepherd, the one permanently selected by Marduk, the exalted ruler."[5] Likewise, the Persian king Cyrus, who captured Babylon in 539 BCE, followed the Babylonian protocol by proclaiming that Marduk had made him king over the whole world after he had "looked throughout all the lands, searching for a righteous king whom he would support."[6]

Not only did rulers proclaim themselves to be divinely chosen, but they also often claimed to be divine themselves. In Egypt, the reigning pharaoh was believed to be divine, the incarnation of either the god Horus or the god Ra. In some other ancient cultures, kings were deified at their death. In Hittite, the language of the dominant population of Asia Minor in the second millennium BCE, the idiom for recounting a royal death was that the king "became a god." We also have evidence for the deification of kings after their death in ancient Canaan. In Rome, Julius Caesar was deified two years after his assassination; when his nephew and adopted son Octavian became emperor and was titled Augustus, one of his titles was *divi filius*, "the son of the divine one." According to the Roman historian Suetonius, the later emperor Vespasian, who was famous for his wit, reportedly said as he was about to die, "Alas! I think I am becoming a god!"[7]

Sometimes in the ancient Near East, kings were also given the title "son of god," probably indicating that they were symbolically adopted as such at their coronation.[8] We find evidence for such a ceremonial adoption in Psalm 2, an ancient Israelite coronation hymn, in which Yahweh announces, probably through a priest or a prophet:

I have installed my king
on Zion, my holy mountain.

The king reports:

> I will tell of Yahweh's decree:
>> He said to me: "You are my son;
>> today I have become your father."
> (Psalm 2:6–7)[9]

Other scriptural texts reinforced the notion that kings, and later even elected leaders, had been divinely chosen. The pseudonymous author of the Wisdom of Solomon reminds kings: "Dominion was given to you by the Lord, and power by the Most High" (6:3).[10] Similarly, the apostle Paul admonished the Christian community in Rome: "There is no authority except from God, and those authorities that exist have been established by God. Therefore, whoever resists authority resists what God has appointed" (Romans 13:1–2).[11]

Following some of these well-established precedents, the medieval Frankish ruler Charlemagne also claimed that he had been divinely chosen. Here is a standard titulature, incorporating in part titles used by earlier Roman emperors: "Charles, the most serene Augustus, crowned by God, the great and peaceful emperor, governing the Roman Empire, who also by the mercy of God is King of the Franks and the Lombards."[12]

We find a similar claim of divine choice on the title page of the "Great Bible," promulgated by Henry VIII of England in 1539.[13] The elaborate woodcut is dominated by the king himself, who is giving the Bible—the word of God—both to his clergy, led by Thomas Cranmer, the archbishop of Canterbury, and to his nobles, led by Thomas Cromwell, the principal royal minister.[14] They pass it on to the king's subjects, who are saying, "Vivat rex" ("Long live the king!") and "God save the kynge!" Above the king, at the top of the illustration, in a kind of time-lapse flashback, Christ proclaims to the king, who is kneeling and not yet crowned, "I have found a man after my heart, who does all that I wish."[15]

In 1806, Emperor Napoleon I required all the churches of his empire to use the same catechism for religious instruction. In the section on the Fourth Commandment ("Honor your father and your mother"), the *Catéchisme impérial* asserts:

> God, who has created empires and distributes them according to his will, has, by loading our emperor with gifts both in peace and in war, established him as our sovereign and made him the agent of his power and his image upon earth. To honor and serve our emperor is therefore to honor and serve God himself.[16]

The *Catéchisme* further claimed that Napoleon "has become the anointed of the Lord by the consecration which he has received from the sovereign pontiff, head of the Church universal."[17] In fact, although Pope Pius VII attended Napoleon's coronation in 1804, he did not crown him emperor—Napoleon put the crown on his own head.

Why has the claim of divine choice been so important for rulers in so many times and so many places? If a ruler can get his or her subjects to accept the notion of a divine right, that he or she is divinely chosen, or shares divinity, or is en route to divinity, or is actually divine, then that would enhance his or her power over them. Insurrection and rebellion would in effect be blasphemous. I venture that no one today thinks that the sun god Shamash chose Hammurapi as king, or that Marduk, the chief god of Babylon, chose Nebuchadrezzar and Cyrus. And few would believe God personally selected Charlemagne, Henry VIII, and Napoleon as rulers. It seems obvious that the raison d'être of their claims was political and did not correspond to actual divine choice.

The words that Christ proclaims to Henry on the title page of the Great Bible are a quotation, or rather a misquotation, from a speech supposedly given by Paul in the synagogue in Antioch in Pisidia, a region in modern-day central Turkey.[18] Paul begins the speech by summarizing the history of Israel from God's choice of their ancestors in Genesis to the time of the prophet Samuel. He then proceeds:

> They asked for a king, and God gave them Saul, the son of Kish, a man from the tribe of Benjamin, for forty years; and after he had

removed him, he raised up David for them as king, about whom he testified, "I have found David, the son of Jesse, a man after my heart, who will do all that I wish." (Acts 13:21–22)

Like Henry later, Paul is inexactly quoting scripture. "A man after my heart" is from Samuel's announcement to Saul, Israel's first king, that God has rejected him:

> Your kingship will not endure. Yahweh has sought for himself a man after his heart, and Yahweh will appoint him as leader over his people. For you have not done what Yahweh commanded you. (1 Samuel 13:14)

At this point in the narrative, David, Saul's ultimate successor as king, has not yet been introduced. Paul collapses the narrative and attaches to Samuel's pronouncement words from Psalm 89, in which Yahweh himself is quoted:

> *"I have found David, my servant;*
> *with my holy oil I have anointed him."*
> (Psalm 89:20)

Then he adds the phrase "who will do all that I wish," from Isaiah 44:28. There it is not about Saul or David, but rather about the Persian king Cyrus. Paul goes on to preach about Jesus, one of David's descendants, quoting as part of his "good news" the words from Psalm 2, "You are my son; today I have become your father."

That Paul interprets an Old Testament text as referring to Jesus is unsurprising; early Christian writers believed (as do many Christians today) that on one level at least the Jewish scriptures were prophecy, finally fulfilled in the person of Jesus of Nazareth. The Great Bible's misquotation of Acts is unsurprising as well: because the Bible was believed to be the direct word of God, verses could be taken from their contexts and applied to almost any situation. Of course, in the original contexts of these quoted and misquoted passages from the

Old Testament, the chosen ruler was not Jesus or Henry VIII, but Saul, David, one of David's successors, or even Cyrus.

David himself is the quintessential biblical example of a divinely chosen ruler, or rather one who claimed to be so. David was Israel's second king, succeeding Saul after Saul's death in battle with the Philistines. That much is historically likely. Yet David's claim to the throne was tenuous. He had been a member of Saul's army and was married to Saul's daughter Michal, but he was not Saul's son and thus not in the line of succession. In the biblical narrative about Saul and David in 1 Samuel, we see two different perspectives. In the first, Saul is depicted positively, as a military leader selected by popular acclaim to be king, despite the opposition of the leader of the old establishment, Samuel. In this pro-Saul narrative, a reluctant Samuel follows divine instructions and designates Saul as the one whom Yahweh himself has chosen. Intertwined with this narrative, however, is a second one, which is a prolonged rationalization for David's succeeding Saul. In this pro-David narrative, Yahweh rejects Saul in favor of David, and that choice, too, is ratified by Yahweh through Samuel. Saul— we are tendentiously told—had disobeyed divine commands and David became the divinely chosen ruler. Many scholars, including me, think that both perspectives were concocted as a myth of divine approval for the assumption of kingship—first by Saul and then by David, a usurper with no real claim to the throne.[19]

In the second perspective, it is supposedly the hero David who defeats the Philistine champion Goliath, although an almost certainly more reliable text attributes that defeat to Elhanan, an otherwise unknown warrior.[20] David is described as more successful than Saul in battle;[21] as one who while on the run from an obsessed Saul twice passes up the opportunity to kill him;[22] and who after Saul's death eulogizes him extravagantly.[23] After he has assumed the throne, David continues to be singled out. It is David to whom Yahweh reportedly says, in language recalling that used by Hammurapi and other ancient rulers, "You will shepherd my people Israel" (2 Samuel 5:2).[24] It is David to whom Yahweh reportedly promises, "Your house and your kingdom will be secure forever before me, and your throne will be established forever" (2 Samuel 7:16).

David, or his successors, elaborated on these supposed divine promises, most fully in Psalm 89. This hymn draws on the myth also found in Enuma Elish. Yahweh's choice of David is linked with divine control over the primeval watery forces of chaos, beginning with their defeat in olden times, and with the creation of the world that followed the victory. The psalmist proclaims to the deity:

> *You rule the sea's arrogance;*
> > *when its waves rise, you calm them.*
> *You crushed Rahab like a corpse;*
> > *with your strong arm you scattered your enemies.*
> *Yours are the heavens, and yours is the earth as well:*
> > *you founded the world and all that fills it.*
> > (Psalm 89:9–11)[25]

In the next part of the psalm, Yahweh himself is quoted:

> *"I have set a crown on a warrior;*
> > *I have elevated one chosen from the people;*
> *I have found David, my servant;*
> > *with my holy oil I have anointed him. . . .*
> *I will set his hand on the sea,*
> > *and his right hand on the rivers.*
> *He will call me 'My father,*
> > *my god, and the rock of my salvation.'*
> *I will make him the firstborn,*
> > *the most high of the kings of the earth.*
> *Forever I will keep my steadfast love toward him,*
> > *and my covenant with him will stand firm:*
> *I will establish his seed forever,*
> > *and his throne like the days of the heavens."*
> > (Psalm 89:19–20, 25–29)

We see familiar motifs here. As with Hammurapi, David's rule is linked with a divinely established order. Here the creator, Yahweh, delegates his ongoing task of controlling primeval chaos to the king: "I will set his hand on the sea." This king, personally chosen and anointed by Yahweh, has a father-son relationship with him, and is designated "firstborn" over other kings. In the propagandistic legends of 1 Samuel, David is the youngest of eight sons of Jesse, but once again, as with Isaac and Jacob, God chooses the youngest son, and raises him to firstborn status.[26] Finally, in this psalm the promise of an unending dynasty is recalled: the psalm goes on to say that David's "seed"—his dynasty—will last forever, like the sun and the moon.

Furthermore, just as the gods supposedly chose not only Hammurapi but also Babylon, so, too, did Yahweh supposedly choose not only David but also his capital city, Jerusalem, often called Zion, especially in poetic texts: "Yahweh chose Zion; he desired it as his dwelling place" (Psalm 132:13). As the divine home, Zion was thought to be invincible—no "foe or enemy could enter the gates of Jerusalem" (Lamentations 4:12). Like David's dynasty, it was also thought to be eternal—"this is my resting place forever" (Psalm 132:14).

But did Yahweh really choose Jerusalem? Not according to one early source, which describes the takeover of the city. On his own initiative, rather than in response to a divine command, David captured it early in his reign and made it his capital. Why? As a non-Israelite city,[27] it had no connection with any of the twelve tribes, so its primary loyalty was to him: it became "the city of David" (2 Samuel 5:7). Centrally situated between the northern and the southern Israelite tribes, it had relatively easy access for all. The reasons for the move to Jerusalem, then, were political, similar to the choice of the District of Columbia as the capital of the young United States of America in 1790, because of its central location and its neutrality outside the boundaries of any state. Then, to further enhance his dubious claim to rule, David brought Yahweh's movable throne, the ark of the covenant, there.[28] The city of David became the city of God by royal act, not by divine decision.

Still, the notion of divine choice of Zion caught hold; centuries later, when Jerusalem was under attack by the Assyrians, the prophet Isaiah reportedly proclaimed: "Thus says Yahweh: '. . . I will protect this city to save it, for my own sake and for the sake of David, my servant'" (2 Kings 19:34). Just as the notion of divine choice of the Israelites justified their sense of superiority to others, not chosen, so too the notion of divine choice of David and his capital city benefited David and his successors most of all. In the process, the Israelites' ancient traditions were coopted. Now Yahweh had a covenant with David; in it, David replaced Israel as Yahweh's firstborn son and Zion replaced Sinai as the mountain of revelation.

In a scene near the end of David's life and reminiscent of Isaac's blessing of Jacob, Bathsheba colluded with other members of the royal court to persuade the aged, impotent, and probably senile king to name Solomon, David's and her son, as his father's successor, outmaneuvering David's oldest surviving son, Adonijah. Solomon soon reportedly claimed that he had been chosen to be king by Yahweh—even though the narrative of Solomon's coronation makes no mention of this—in an apparently effective counter to his having bypassed the conventional line of succession: "Yahweh, my god, you made your servant king in place of David, my father" (1 Kings 3:7). Even Adonijah seems to have recognized this claim, when he said to Bathsheba, concerning Solomon, "You know that the kingship belonged to me, and also Israel expected me to become king, but the kingship has turned round and has become my brother's, for it was his from Yahweh" (1 Kings 2:15). This acknowledgment did not prevent Solomon from having him executed early in his reign.

During much of the tenth century BCE under David and Solomon, Israel was a united kingdom. But soon after Solomon died it split into two kingdoms, Judah in the south and Israel in the north. From then on, most biblical sources come from Judah, where for some three and a half centuries kings in David's line continued to rule from Jerusalem. These sources are almost uniformly hostile to the northern kingdom, a hostility that is expressed in the claim that God had solely chosen Judah along with the Davidic dynasty and its capital Jerusalem, not its northern neighbor Israel. For example, a psalmist will assert that Yahweh "rejected . . . Joseph, and did not choose the tribe of Ephraim. He chose the tribe of Judah, Mount Zion, which he loves" (Psalm 78:67–68). From the biased perspective of the southern kingdom of Judah, the north—often called Ephraim after Jacob's son Joseph's younger, favored son—was no longer part of the chosen people.

Subsequent events seemed to confirm this assertion. Some two centuries after its split with the southern kingdom of Judah, the northern kingdom of Israel was conquered by the Assyrians. From the Judean perspective, as set forth at length in the book of Kings, this was because the northern Israelites had worshiped gods other than Yahweh and had engaged in forbidden rituals:

> They abandoned all the commands of Yahweh, their god, and they made for themselves molten images . . . ; and they made an Asherah, and they worshipped all the army of heaven, and they served Baal.[29] And they made their sons and their daughters pass through fire, and they practiced divination and sorcery, and they sold themselves to do evil in the eyes of Yahweh to provoke him. So Yahweh was very angry with Israel, and he removed them from his presence. Only the tribe of Judah was left. . . . Yahweh rejected all the seed of Israel, and he afflicted them by giving them into the hands of plunderers, until he had expelled them from his presence. (2 Kings 17:16–20)

This theological explanation ignores the historical reality: Assyria's imperial power eliminated the northern kingdom of Israel, a small nation that stood in the way of its intended conquest of Egypt, while leaving more or less intact (for the time being at least) the even smaller and more remote kingdom of Judah, which was no real threat to their ambitions. But no matter: from the Judean perspective, the supposedly divinely instigated destruction of their northern rival proved that only they were still chosen. The tribes that had constituted the northern kingdom, despite their genealogical roots back to

Jacob's sons, had been rejected; they became the "ten lost tribes" of history and legend. Once again, divine choice had been narrowed, purportedly by God himself.

Judah and its capital survived attacks and sieges for more than a century after the fall of the northern kingdom.[30] But in the end history proved its extravagant claims wrong. Jerusalem, it turned out, was not impregnable: in 586 BCE, after a siege of more than a year, the Babylonians, who had succeeded the Assyrians as imperial rulers of the Near East, captured Jerusalem. Yahweh's own house, the temple that Solomon had built, was ransacked and burned, and much of the population was deported to Babylon. The last descendant of David to sit on the throne, Zedekiah, caught as he tried to flee, was forced to witness the execution of his sons before he was blinded. The dynasty had lasted some four centuries—a long run, as dynasties go, but hardly forever.

The human agent of the catastrophe was the Babylonian ruler Nebuchadrezzar.[31] Biblical writers again had their own spin. According to the prophet Jeremiah, Nebuchadrezzar was the servant of Yahweh, not of the Babylonian god Marduk, and it was Yahweh who was using the Babylonians to punish the people of Judah.[32] Biblical writers thus explained the fall of Jerusalem, the end of the Davidic dynasty, and Nebuchadrezzar's deportation of Judeans to Babylon much as they had explained the defeat of the northern kingdom of Israel: divinely imposed punishment for breaking covenant commandments, especially by worshipping other gods. One of those writers, the prophet Jeremiah, an eyewitness to Jerusalem's destruction, connected the two disasters, speaking in Yahweh's name:

> Because you are doing all these things: . . . when I spoke to you persistently, you did not listen, and when I called to you, you did not answer, therefore I will do to the house that is called by my name, in which you trust, and to the place that I gave to you and to your fathers, just as I did to Shiloh.[33] And I will cast you out of my presence, just as I cast out all your brothers, all the seed of Ephraim. (Jeremiah 7:13–15)

For Jeremiah, despite the royal propaganda, Judah's chosen status was conditional rather than eternal, as also was the chosen status of Jerusalem and of the dynasty founded by David.

■ ■ ■

CLEARLY ONE THEME that pervades much of biblical literature from the monarchic period is the Israelites' special, even unique status as chosen by Yahweh. The prophet Amos put it this way, speaking in Yahweh's name: "You only have I known of all the families of the earth." echoing both Yahweh's special knowledge of Abraham and the sexual metaphor of his covenant relationship with the Israelites with the verb "to know" in the biblical sense, as the saying goes.[34] But that verse occurs in a context of condemnation and judgment:

> Hear this word which Yahweh has spoken against you, O sons of Israel, against the whole family that I brought up out of the land of Egypt:
>
> *You only have I known of all the families of the earth;*
> *therefore I will punish you for all your iniquities.*
> (Amos 3:1–2)

As his chosen people, the Israelites had a special, even intimate relationship with Yahweh, a relationship that entailed obligations that had to be lived up to. If the Israelites failed to do so, Yahweh would punish them. The prophets, along with ancient Israel's historians, interpreted foreign attacks on Israel and even its defeat and eventually exile as punishments inflicted by Yahweh.

The actual agents of the punishments, however, were foreign powers, especially Assyria, Babylonia, and Egypt, as well as from time to time Israel's nearer neighbors, such as the Philistines and the Arameans. From one theological perspective, these other nations were simply instruments used by Yahweh. Isaiah describes Assyria as the rod of Yahweh's anger, the weapon in his hands directed against his

people.[35] Implicit in this understanding is a monotheistic development: Yahweh was not just the god of Israel, but of all the world; he
was, as some modern interpreters have put it, "the lord of history."
As such, he controlled not just Israel, but other nations too. According to an anonymous prophet, Cyrus, the king of Persia, had actually
been chosen by Yahweh as his "shepherd . . . his anointed" (Isaiah
44:28–45:1), even though he himself announced that he had been
chosen by Marduk to replace the Babylonian king Nabonidus as ruler
of Babylon. From the perspective of Judean exiles in Babylon, Yahweh
was using Cyrus both to punish the Babylonians for what they had
done to Jerusalem and to return the exiles to Zion; Yahweh's primary
interest lay with "my servant Jacob, Israel my chosen one" (Isaiah
45:4). But was this necessarily so?

At times, some biblical writers offer a different, more inclusive
view. Just because the Israelites were chosen, were loved, did not
mean that others were not. If Yahweh is the lord of all, should not he
then be equally concerned with all? Indeed, says the prophet Amos,
again speaking in Yahweh's name:

Are not you like the sons of the Cushites to me, O sons of Israel?
   Did I not bring Israel up from the land of Egypt,
   and the Philistines from Caphtor, and Aram from Kir?[36]
   (Amos 9:7)

The Israelites, according to Amos, were not so special: Yahweh was
just as attached to the distant Cushites as he was to them. He had
guided the migrations of the Philistines and the Arameans just as he
had brought the Israelites out of Egypt. A similar perspective is found
in Isaiah, who announces:

Israel will be the third with Egypt and with Assyria, a blessing
in the midst of the earth, whom Yahweh of armies has blessed:
"Blessed be my people Egypt, and Assyria the work of my hands,
and Israel my inheritance." (Isaiah 19:24–25)

In these and only a few other passages, we find an alternative to self-promoting national exceptionalism. Again, however, just because we find such more inclusive passages more congenial, does that make them more authoritative? It is wrong, I think, to consider only some of the words attributed to the deity actual revelation and others as mere human creations, when really they are all human creations. And it would be naïve at best to assume that any Assyrian, Egyptian, or Persian ruler would be inclined to worship Yahweh, despite self-centered texts such as this:

> In future days,
> the mountain of Yahweh's house will be established
>   at the top of the mountains,
>   raised higher than the hills.
> And all the nations will stream toward it,
>   and many peoples will come and they will say,
> "Let us go up to Yahweh's mountain,
>   to the house of the god of Jacob,
> so that he may teach us his ways
>   and we may walk in his paths."
> For from Zion teaching will go out,
>   and Yahweh's word from Jerusalem.[37]
>   (Isaiah 2:2–3)[38]

Words such as these are addressed to Israelite and ancient Jewish audiences, who continued to wrestle with the issue of chosenness. The tone is inclusive and universal, but God's original chosen ones, now reduced to the Judeans, were still in their own view unique, and they fantasized that their capital city would be the goal of pilgrimage for all nations. Inclusivity and universalism can be politically self-serving, not just politically correct.

5

WHICH SURVIVORS
WERE CHOSEN?

THE BABYLONIAN DESTRUCTION OF JERUSALEM and the exile of many of Judah's inhabitants to Babylonia in the early sixth century BCE was a national trauma for the Israelites. The temple Yahweh had reportedly said was his home lay in ruins. David's dynasty, supposedly eternally chosen, had come to an abrupt end. The Israelites had lost control of the land they believed Yahweh had promised to them. Only a fraction of the population—a remnant—remained there.

The concept of a remnant—expressed by a cluster of Hebrew words that mean not just those remaining but also escapees and survivors—has two connotations in the Bible, especially in the books of the prophets. One is negative: Yahweh's punishment both of the Israelites for breaking their covenant with him and of their enemies will be so severe that only a negligible few will be spared. So, Amos predicts of the elite in Samaria, the capital of the northern kingdom of Israel:

> As a shepherd rescues from the lion's mouth
> two shins or a piece of an ear,
> so will the Israelites living in Samaria be rescued.
>   (Amos 3:12)

Likewise, Isaiah says of the Moabites that their "remnant will be tiny, not strong" (Isaiah 16:14), and Jeremiah proclaims of the Jerusalem establishment, "Death will be preferable to life for all the remaining remnant of this evil family" (Jeremiah 8:3).

More frequently in the Bible, however, "remnant" has a positive connotation, referring to a now-purified group of survivors after divine punishment. In the context of the earlier Assyrian advance on Israel and Judah in the late eighth century BCE, Isaiah gave one of his sons the symbolic name Shear-jashub, which means "A remnant will return" (Isaiah 7:3), personifying the prophet's message that the coming devastation would not be total.[1] Isaiah's contemporary Micah proclaimed:

> *Who is a god like you,*
> *   taking away transgression*
> *and passing over the rebellion*
> *   of the remnant of his inheritance?* . . .
> *You will show faithfulness* . . .
> *as you swore to our fathers*
> *   in days of old.*
> (Micah 7:18, 20)

Passages such as this are difficult to date because they lack specifics; that may be one reason they were preserved, because they can apply to different historical contexts. While the passage would certainly fit in Micah's own context in late eighth-century BCE Judah, it could equally well apply to subsequent periods. No matter when it was written, however, the passage expresses confidence that Yahweh will continue to keep his ancient promises to those of his people who remain, despite their frequent transgressions.

But this introduces another problem, that of divine justice, or theodicy in academic jargon. Consider this ancient liturgical anthem, echoed in Micah and in more than a dozen other passages, including the Ten Commandments:

> *Yahweh, Yahweh,*
> *a loving and kind god,*
> *slow to be angry,*
> *and abounding in loving-kindness and faithfulness,*

showing loving-kindness to the thousandth generation,
taking away transgression and rebellion and sin.
Yet he does not acquit the guilty,
but punishes for the transgression of fathers
sons and sons' sons
to the third and fourth generation.
　　(Exodus 34:6–7)[2]

Like many of his ancient counterparts, Yahweh is described as a just deity who rewards the good and their offspring, and punishes the wicked and their offspring. But also like other gods, he forgives both the wicked and their offspring. Those who prosper are righteous (or at least their forebears were), as their prosperity shows, and those who suffer are necessarily guilty (or at least their forebears were), as their suffering shows. The survivors of divine judgment, the remnant, can therefore be viewed as those spared by divine mercy, and therefore implicitly righteous as well. But experience suggests otherwise. As recognized by the authors of Job and Ecclesiastes as well as some non-biblical writers, there is no simple correlation between living a moral life and being happy and prosperous, nor does living an immoral life inevitably result in experiencing hardship and an early death. Ecclesiastes puts it this way: "A sinner does wrong a hundred times, but has a long life" (8:12).

Moreover, the repeated formula itself has inconsistencies. Does God forgive wrongdoing or punish it? If a deity is not forgiving, what hope do sinners have? And why would a just deity punish children, grandchildren, and great-grandchildren for the wrongdoing of their parents? The trauma of 586 BCE prompted such questions.

The deportation of Judeans to Babylonia in 586 BCE by King Nebuchadrezzar was not the first deportation. A decade earlier, he had laid siege to Jerusalem, but relented when the Judean king, Jehoiachin, surrendered. Jehoiachin and his court, along with several thousand other Judeans, were taken captive and exiled to Babylon; others fled to Egypt. Nebuchadrezzar replaced Jehoiachin with his uncle Zedekiah, who ruled those remaining in Judah until the fall of Jerusalem in 586. Tensions soon developed between those in exile—the Babylonian Diaspora—and those still in Judah. According to the book of Ezekiel, named for the priest-prophet who himself had been deported in 597, those still in Judah wrongly claimed that Yahweh was punishing the exiles, who had broken his covenant by worshipping other gods, with the curses of dispossession and deportation that were part of the covenant's formulary. Continued possession of the Promised Land by those who had not been exiled showed, they asserted, that they were blameless.[3] But Ezekiel, one of the exiles himself, insisted that Yahweh was with those who had been deported, not with those left in Judah, who were continuing their idolatrous practices. He reports having been shown in a vision how "the glory of Yahweh," the divine presence, left the temple in Jerusalem and headed east, to join his people in Babylonia. In the prophet's view, Yahweh was no longer in the Promised Land, but with the exiles.[4]

This was not just Ezekiel's view. His contemporary, the prophet Jeremiah, who remained in Judah for several years after Jerusalem's destruction, also reports a symbolic vision, in which Yahweh showed him two baskets, one of good figs and one of bad, inedible figs. Yahweh identifies the bad figs as "Zedekiah, the king of Judah, and his princes and the remnant of Jerusalem who remain in this land," and says that he will eliminate them from the Promised Land (Jeremiah 24:8–10). But the good figs are the Judean exiles in Babylonia, who will eventually return to Judah.[5] Jeremiah and Ezekiel agree: only the exiles are Yahweh's people; those left in Judah are not.

Some prophets in Jerusalem after the 597 deportation had predicted that within two years Nebuchadrezzar would be defeated and the exiles would return. But the prophet Jeremiah accused them of being false prophets. Speaking in Yahweh's name, he reportedly wrote to the exiles directly, reversing the alliterative words of the psalmist "Sha'alu shalom yerushalaim" ("Ask for the peace of Jerusalem," Psalm 122:6) with "Seek the peace of the city to which I have exiled you, and pray for it to Yahweh, for in its peace will be your peace" (Jeremiah 29:7). There would be no return in the foreseeable future: the exiles should make Babylon their home.

Tensions between those in the Diaspora and those living in the Promised Land continued for centuries and have had reverberations down to the present.[6] Here we will focus on the two centuries immediately after 586 BCE. The exiles in Babylonia, seeing themselves as the chosen remnant, developed the fiction that the land had been made empty, and that they—like the Israelites under Moses—would have a new Exodus and take possession of the land that Yahweh had given to them and only them. We find the assertion that the land was empty in many biblical books written after 586 BCE. For example, at the end of the books of Chronicles, which probably date to the fifth or fourth century BCE, we are told that Nebuchadrezzar

> exiled to Babylon those who had survived the sword, and they became his and his sons' servants until the kingdom of Persia ruled, to fulfill the word of Yahweh from the mouth of Jeremiah, until the land had enjoyed its sabbaths. All the days that it was desolate it kept sabbath, to fulfill seventy years. (2 Chronicles 36:20–21)

The author of Chronicles is combining ideas taken from the earlier books of Jeremiah and Leviticus. Jeremiah or one of his later editors had prophesied that "the whole land will become a ruin and a desolation" (25:11), "without humans or animals" (33:12), and that the Judeans and their neighbors would "serve the king of Babylon for seventy years" (25:11; see also 29:10).[7] Leviticus connects this with the Israelites' failure to observe the sabbatical years:

> I will scatter you among the nations, and I will unsheathe the sword against you. Your land will be a desolation, and your cities will be in ruins. . . . As long as the land is desolate, it will have the rest it did not have on your sabbaths when you were living on it. (Leviticus 26:33, 35)[8]

The punishment fits the crime: seventy years of the land not being cultivated, in retribution for the Israelites' failure to let it lie fallow every seventh year as required by ancient law.[9]

Both Jeremiah and Leviticus draw on the ancient idea that Yahweh would punish the Israelites if they did not keep their covenant with him. In the book of Deuteronomy, the punishments for breaking the covenant include both dispossession and exile:

> If you do not carefully observe all the words of this law, . . . then Yahweh will delight in destroying you and making you perish, and you will be plucked out of the land that you are entering to possess. And Yahweh will scatter you among all the nations, from one end of the earth to the other. (Deuteronomy 28:58, 63–64)

These texts, and others like them, are prophecy after the fact: that the Promised Land became uninhabited after 586 BCE reflects the perspective of the exiles in Babylonia.[10]

The notion of an empty land, however, is hyperbole, a literary construct rather than actual reality. Both textual and archaeological evidence make it clear that some people continued to live in Judah after Jerusalem's destruction, although the population was significantly smaller, perhaps only a third of what it had been.[11] But especially after yet another deportation in 582 BCE,[12] the locus of power within the broader Judean community had shifted. By their own definition at least, the exiles, and only they, were the chosen people.

The books of Chronicles close on a positive note, quoting a decree of Cyrus, the king of Persia, dated to the first year after his capture of Babylon in 539 BCE:

> Yahweh, the god of heaven, has given me all the kingdoms of the earth, and he charged me to build him a house in Jerusalem, which is in Judah. Whoever is among you of all his people, may Yahweh his god be with him, and let him go up. (2 Chronicles 36:23)[13]

Scholars debate whether this decree is authentic, but at least its substance may be accurate, as well as its date, 538 BCE. Just as Cyrus had claimed, for a Babylonian audience, that their god Marduk had given him rule over Babylon, so now he claims, for a Judean audience in exile, that Yahweh had both given him his power and instructed him to rebuild the Jerusalem temple that the Babylonians and Edomites had destroyed. Certainly some among the exiles agreed; here is how one anonymous author put it:

> [Yahweh] says of Jerusalem:
>   "It will be inhabited,"
> and of the cities of Judah:
>   "They will be built,
>   and I will raise up all their ruins. . . ."
> He says of Cyrus: "He is my shepherd;
>   he will carry out everything I wish."
> He says of Jerusalem: "It will be built,
>   and the temple's foundations will be laid."
>   (Isaiah 44:26, 28)

This text, from the latter part of the book of Isaiah, dates to the time of Cyrus rather than to the late eighth century BCE, when the prophet Isaiah lived. For this postexilic writer, the Persian king was Yahweh's "anointed one" (in Hebrew, *mashiach* ["messiah"]), whom he had called "for the sake of my servant Jacob, Israel my chosen one . . . to free my exiles" (Isaiah 45:1, 3–4, 13). Once again, a deity has chosen a king, but now the deity is Yahweh, not Marduk, and the king is not David, but Cyrus, who is now Yahweh's chosen shepherd.

Behind the extravagant poetry, with its notions of an empty land and of Cyrus as Yahweh's anointed ruler, is a historical kernel: the Persian king, likely wanting to establish in the small province of Judah a regime loyal to him, allowed some of the elite who had been deported by the Babylonians to return to Jerusalem. The leaders of the returnees were Jeshua, a high-ranking priest, Zerubbabel, a descendent of David, and Sheshbazzar, a "prince of Judah" (Ezra 1:8), perhaps another member of the Judean royal family. Immediately, they came into conflict with those who had never left.

One early conflict had to do with rebuilding the temple. According to several biblical sources, although the work started soon after the return of the exiles, it was not completed for some twenty years. One reason for the delay, according to Haggai, prophesying in 520 BCE, was that the returned exiles and their leaders were more interested in their own comfort than in full restoration of divine service: "Is it a time for you to live in your paneled houses, while this house is in ruins?" (Haggai 1:4). But the book of Ezra gives another reason. When the initial reconstruction had begun, some of the locals, called "the enemies of Judah and Benjamin," came to the leaders of the returnees and asked:

> "Let us build with you. For like you we worship your god, and we have been sacrificing to him from the days of Esar-haddon, the king of Assyria, who brought us here." (Ezra 4:1–2)

This purported request identifies the speakers not as native-born Judeans but rather as the descendants of foreigners whom the Assyrians had settled in the former northern kingdom of Israel in the late eighth century BCE.[14] The returned exiles, however, rejected this offer of cooperation from these ethnically non-Israelites, even though they were coreligionists:

> "You and we will not build a house to our god; rather, we alone will build for Yahweh the god of Israel, as King Cyrus, the king of Persia, commanded us." (Ezra 4:3)

Then, we are told, the locals, also called "the people of the land," bribed regional Persian officials to prevent the rebuilding of the temple, but those officials wisely checked with their superiors in Persia, who confirmed Cyrus's decree. In this self-serving account, the returned exiles were able to use their close links with the Persian government to set themselves over and apart from other worshippers of Yahweh.

The Bible does not have a continuous history of early postexilic Jewish communities. Rather, we find detailed narratives of specific episodes, focusing mainly on the relationship between Jews from the

Babylonian Diaspora and those who had remained in Judah; we can occasionally supplement the biblical narratives with evidence from nonbiblical sources. This much is clear: Jews, as we may now call them—that is, people who traced their origins back to the kingdom of Judah—were found not only in the Persian province of Judah and its near neighbors, but throughout the Persian empire, in Babylonia, in Egypt, and even in Persia itself.[15] They were linked not only by their origins, but by their continued worship of Yahweh and their observance of Sabbath and Passover. Many also recognized the authority of the priestly establishment in the newly rebuilt temple in Jerusalem.

But that establishment itself was not always so ecumenical. A second conflict between the returned exiles and others in the Promised Land is reported in the mid-fifth century BCE. The Persian-appointed Jewish governor of Judah, Nehemiah, who was also a high official in the court of the Persian king Artaxerxes I, had come with royal authorization to Jerusalem to rebuild its walls. In his memoir, which may well be authentic, Nehemiah reports that his mission was opposed by the local leaders Sanballat the Horonite, Tobiah the Ammonite, and Geshem the Arab. All three are also known from contemporaneous nonbiblical texts. Sanballat was governor of Samaria; Tobiah was in charge of Ammon, east of the Jordan River; and Geshem ruled territory south of Ammon. From their perspective, it seems, Nehemiah's mission was an unwarranted intervention in their regional politics. But in Nehemiah's view, they had "no share, right, or historical link to Jerusalem" (Nehemiah 2:20). Nehemiah goes on to accuse them of plotting to kill him; their coconspirators included some prophets, among them Noadiah, one of four named women prophets in the Bible.[16] This, then, was not really a foreign plot. Moreover, at least two of the principal plotters were Yahwists and were closely connected with the priestly establishment: Sanballat's daughter was married to a son of the high priest, and Tobiah (whose name means "Yahweh is good") was close to the high priest as well and even had private quarters in the temple precinct.

So, nearly a century after the exiles had returned, there continued to be tensions both within Judah and between some in Judah and their near neighbors. Largely, if not entirely, to blame were Persian appointees from the Babylonian Diaspora. Nehemiah and his associate Ezra the priest and scribe sought to impose their authority, especially in matters of religious practice, on the entire population—returnees as well as those who had remained in Judah. Nowhere is this more evident than in the issue of exogamy, marriage outside one's group. When the completion of the repair of Jerusalem's fortifications was being celebrated, during a public reading from "the scroll of Moses . . . it was found written in it that no Ammonite or Moabite should enter the congregation of God forever" (Nehemiah 13:1). The apparently coincidental discovery of this exclusion, found in Deuteronomy 23:3 (odd that it had not been noticed before!), served as a lead-in for Nehemiah's further exclusion of "foreign" worshippers of Yahweh, when he

> saw Jews who had married Ashdodite, Ammonite, and Moabite women. And of their children, half spoke Ashdodite or the language of other peoples, and they could not speak Judahite.[17] So I accused them, and cursed them, and I beat some of the men and I pulled out their hair. I made them swear by God, "You should not give your daughters to their sons, nor should you take their daughters for your sons or for yourselves. . . . So I cleansed them from everything foreign. (Nehemiah 13:23–25, 30)

Ethnic cleansing because of mixed marriages had also been part of the program of Nehemiah's colleague Ezra when he had arrived in Jerusalem a decade or so before Nehemiah became governor. Returned exiles, it seems, had intermarried with those who had not been exiled: "the holy seed has become mixed with the peoples of the lands" (Ezra 9:2). At a solemn assembly, Ezra ordered all the "sons of the exile" to separate themselves "from the peoples of the land and from the foreign women" (Ezra 10:11). After an investigation that lasted two months, more than a hundred men, including priests, Levites, and other temple personnel, were identified as having married "foreign women" with whom they had had children. They all agreed to separate from their wives and children, and both women and children were sent away.[18] The whole episode is reminiscent of Abraham's expulsion of Hagar at Sarah's insistence, and it carried the same horrible consequences: husbands and wives were separated from each other, and children were forcibly separated from their fathers. Significantly, the basis for the exclusion of these "foreign women" and their children was not a supposed divine command, but rather a now-authoritative text, an early form of the Torah, applied by Diaspora purists to a context entirely different from its original one.

Opposition to marriage outside one's group is a widespread cultural phenomenon. Marriage with outsiders dilutes a group's coherence and even its identity. Of my own children's two grandmothers, one was of Sicilian heritage and grew up in an Italian-speaking Catholic home in New York City; the other, my mother, grew up in Wisconsin in a German-speaking Lutheran home. But my children do not identify as Sicilian or German, or Irish (as their last name would suggest), nor as Catholic or Lutheran, nor in fact as anything other than American: they have lost the cultural identities that in many ways defined their grandmothers because those grandmothers married outside their ethnic group, as did my children's mother and I. On the other hand, marriage within a very narrow group—endogamy, the opposite of exogamy—can result in inbreeding with associated genetic disorders. Ancient societies recognized this and most had taboos against incest—the most radical form of endogamy.

Not surprisingly, biblical writers do not have consistent views about intermarriage. Moses's marriage to a Midianite woman, although initially mentioned without comment, is also criticized.[19] The endogamy insisted upon in the books of Ezra and Nehemiah in fifth-century Judea is not characteristic of all literature of the Persian period. Intermarriage between Jews and others is at least tolerated in the book of Esther and even celebrated in the book of Ruth. We also find a much more inclusive attitude toward non-Judean outsiders

in the books of Chronicles and in this passage from the late sixth or
early fifth century BCE, before Ezra and Nehemiah's reform:

> Let not the foreigner, the one joined to Yahweh, say:
> "Yahweh will separate me from his people." . . .
> As for the foreigners who join themselves to Yahweh,
>   to minister to him, and to love Yahweh's name,
>   and to be his servants . . . ,
> their burnt offerings and their sacrifices
>   will be acceptable on my altar.
> For my house will be called
>   a house of prayer for all peoples.
> (Isaiah 56:3, 6–7)

According to this and similar passages, foreigners who choose to
worship Yahweh may be included in his community.[20] But such
intra-Jewish inclusiveness is at odds with the fanatical exclusivity of
Ezra and Nehemiah, who identified their group as the only true Israel,
the chosen remnant.

6

CHRISTIANS AS A NEW CHOSEN PEOPLE

BY THE FIFTH CENTURY BCE, Jewish self-identification as divinely chosen was well established. To be sure, disagreements existed about who belonged to the chosen people and who did not, disagreements that continued in the centuries that followed and remain in the present. Were the chosen those living in the Promised Land, or in the Diaspora, or both? Were only those who strictly observed Jewish ritual and practices chosen or were also those who tried to accommodate their religious observance to the Persian and then the Hellenistic empires whose subjects they were? Were the chosen those whose worship centered on Jerusalem or those who had seceded from the Jerusalem establishment and declared themselves to be the only truly "holy seed"? So varied are the subgroups that developed within the Jewish community as a whole from the sixth century BCE to the first century CE that some scholars have come to speak of Judaisms rather than just Judaism.

Among the various groups that constituted Judaism from the second century BCE through the first century CE, several are familiar from the New Testament and other first-century CE sources. These groups include the Sadducees, the Pharisees, the scribes, the Samaritans, and the Essenes. The history of each of these groups is only incompletely known, but it is clear that none was monolithic, each having its own internal disputes as well as with each other.

The temple establishment was controlled by the Sadducees from the late second century BCE to the fall of Jerusalem to the Romans in 70 CE. Most if not all of the high priests during this period were Sadducees. The Pharisees were a kind of loyal opposition to the Sadducees, and were also a popular movement that emphasized study of the Torah and observance of its laws. The Pharisees are generally considered to be the forebears of rabbinic Judaism. Less is known about the scribes, but they were associated both with the temple establishment and with the Pharisees.

The Samaritans and the Essenes were both groups that separated themselves from the temple establishment, likely in the second century BCE. Located in the former Assyrian province of Samaria, for which they were named, the Samaritans believed that their sacred scripture, the Torah alone, was the only correct version of the teaching of Moses. The "Samaritan Pentateuch," as scholars call it, although close to the traditional Jewish text, contains minor changes to establish that Mount Gerizim, near Shechem, was the only legitimate place to worship Yahweh, rather than Jerusalem.[1] The Samaritan temple there was destroyed by the Jerusalem high priest John Hyrcanus in about 110 BCE, an action that seems to have crystallized the antagonism between Samaritans and the temple establishment; each group regarded the other as heretical and not authentically Jewish.[2] A community of about eight hundred Samaritans still survives in Israel and Palestine.

The Essenes are best known because of the Dead Sea Scrolls. In the mid-twentieth century, hundreds of texts were found near one of their settlements, whose modern Arabic name is Qumran, on the northwest side of the Dead Sea. Many of these texts are important early manuscripts of the books of the Hebrew Bible (all of which are represented, except perhaps coincidentally for the book of Esther). From some of the Essenes' own sectarian writings we learn that they had fled into the wilderness in secession from the Jerusalem establishment, which in their view was led by a "wicked priest," probably Jonathan, the youngest of the Maccabee brothers, who was high priest from 153 to 143 BCE. At Qumran, under their leader, "the teacher of righteousness," whose historical identity is uncertain, the Essenes were preparing the way of the Lord in the wilderness.[3] They expected a triumph of the forces of light over those of darkness in a not-too-distant end-time and thought of themselves—and only themselves—as "God's chosen."[4] The Essenes, at Qumran at least, seem to have been eliminated during the First Jewish Revolt against Rome (66–73 BCE), after they had stashed their sacred texts in several caves near their settlement, where the scrolls remained until their discovery beginning in the late 1940s.

In the first century CE, another Jewish group formed, whose adherents soon claimed that now they were God's chosen. Like their predecessors and contemporaries, they made use of older biblical language in support of their claim. Decades later, this Jewish movement became known as "Christians," being named by their Roman detractors as followers of an insurrectionist leader, Jesus of Nazareth, who had been executed by the Romans in about 30 CE. His followers believed that he was the anointed one, the Messiah—in Greek, *Christos*—and that he would soon return "to judge the living and the dead" (2 Timothy 4:1).[5]

Initially, the early followers of Jesus were just another movement under the larger umbrella of Judaism. These members of the Jesus movement—sometimes called "Jewish Christians," or perhaps better "Christian Jews"—worshipped both in the temple in Jerusalem and in synagogues everywhere, observed the Sabbath and dietary laws, and practiced circumcision. The Jewish scriptures were their holy text. But as the movement rapidly grew to include non-Jews—Gentiles—the question began to be asked whether one had to observe all the requirements of the Torah in order to be Christian. Some, led it seems by Jesus's brother James, insisted that they did: Christians, all Christians, were still Jews.

The earliest and probably the most reliable statement of James's view is in the apostle Paul's letter to the scattered Christian communities in Galatia, in what is now northern Turkey. Writing around 50 CE, only about twenty years after the death of Jesus, Paul, who identified himself as an observant Jew and as a Pharisee, reports that representatives from James had come to Galatia and insisted that Gentile Christians there should keep Jewish dietary laws and practice circumcision.[6] Although Paul angrily denounces this demand, it endured for several decades.[7] It is prominent in the Gospel of Matthew, generally thought to have been written by a Jewish Christian late in the first century. In it we find Jesus speaking about Torah observance in the Sermon on the Mount:

> Do not think that I have come to abolish the Law and the Prophets: I have not come to abolish but to fulfill. Amen I say to you, until heaven and earth pass away, not one iota or one stroke of a letter will pass away from the Law, until everything has taken place.[8] So whoever annuls one of the least of these commandments and teaches people to do so will be called least in the kingdom of heaven. But whoever obeys and teaches them will be called great in the kingdom of heaven. (Matthew 5:17–19)

It is impossible not to read this as an attack on those who, like Paul, held more relaxed views about strict Torah observance by Gentiles.

We also find in the Gospel of Matthew Jesus apparently instructing his disciples to spread his message only to Jews:

> Do not travel on a road to the Gentiles, and do not enter a city of the Samaritans; rather go only to the lost sheep of the house of Israel. (Matthew 10:5–6; see also 15:21–28)

According to Matthew, Jesus was not "a prophet to the nations" like Jeremiah (1:5) or Jonah. Rather, like most other Israelite prophets, his primary mission was to his fellow Jews. The same Gospel has other pejorative references to Gentiles, such as this:

> When you pray, do not repeat words as the Gentiles do; for they think that they will be heard because of their many words. (Matthew 6:7; see also 5:47)

It seems clear, then, that for Matthew, being a follower of Jesus entailed being Jewish, and non-Jews—Gentiles—were somehow inferior.

Paul had a different view. For him, the Jews continued to be God's chosen people: "God has not rejected his people whom he knew beforehand" (Romans 11:2). But Paul also thought that Gentile Christians as well would be saved through their faith in Jesus.[9] They had been grafted, as it were, onto the tree of Judaism, so that among believers there was no longer any distinction between Jews and Gentiles.[10] Paul was adamant that that did not mean that Gentiles had to become Jews and be circumcised (probably the main issue for adult male converts), despite what James and other Jewish Christians maintained. To the Galatians he wrote that he wished those seeking to impose circumcision on them would castrate themselves.[11]

Eventually, however, Paul's view that Gentile Christians had been grafted onto the tree of Judaism, that God's people were one, was radically altered. The destruction of Jerusalem and its temple by the Romans in 70 CE apparently proved that the Jews were no longer God's chosen people. They had rejected Jesus, whom God had sent to them, so God had rejected them. We find this implied in the earliest Gospel, Mark. Using the frequent biblical allegory of Israel as God's vineyard,[12] the Gospel of Mark has Jesus tell this story to the religious establishment in the temple itself:[13]

> A man planted a vineyard, put a fence around it, dug out a wine press, built a tower, leased it to farmers, and went abroad. In due time, he sent a slave to the farmers to get his share of the vineyard's fruit from them. But they grabbed him and beat him and sent him away empty-handed. Then he sent another slave to them, but they beat him on the head and insulted him. Then he sent another and they killed him, and many others, some of whom they beat, and others they killed. He still had one more, a beloved son. Finally he sent him to them, saying, "They will respect my son." But those farmers said to each other, "This one is the heir. Come, let us kill him, and the inheritance will be

ours." So they grabbed him and killed him and threw him outside the vineyard.

What will the owner of the vineyard do? He will come and destroy the farmers, and he will give the vineyard to others. Do you not know this scripture:

> *"The stone that the builders rejected*
> *has become the capstone;*
> *by the Lord this was done,*
> *and it is amazing in our eyes"?*
> (Mark 12:1–11)

In the parable, the vineyard is Israel, God's possession. But those to whom he entrusted its care were rapacious, constantly mistreating the messengers God sent to them and even killing his son. So he will remove them from power and turn the vineyard over to others. The sense of the allegory was clear to Jesus's audience, the temple establishment: "They recognized that he had spoken this parable against them" (Mark 12:12).

The passage dates not only to after the death of Jesus, which it predicts after the fact, but also likely to after the Roman destruction of Jerusalem in 70 CE. The "others" to whom the vineyard is to be given are not identified; they may well be Christians, both Jews and Gentiles. The quotation at the end of the parable is from Psalm 118, and it became a kind of proof text for early Christians. No matter that originally it had nothing to do with God's rejection of the Jews: in the psalm it is a joyous expression of surprise from a community when a petitioner, perhaps a king, is thanking God for having saved him from trouble. For most Christian writers and thinkers until modernity, everything in the Old Testament, including this psalm verse, is in some sense about Jesus.

In addition to its occurrence in the parable of the vineyard, the same verse is quoted in Acts of the Apostles. The apostle Peter is defending himself before the high priest and other temple officials.

He has just healed a man who had been lame from birth, and is explaining how he did so:

> in the name of Jesus Christ the Nazorean whom you crucified. . . .
> He is
>
>> *"the stone despised by you, the builders,*
>>   *that became the capstone."*
>
> In no one else is there salvation, nor is there any other name under heaven given among men by which we must be saved. (Acts 4:10–12)

In this elaboration of the psalm's verse, the rejected individual is explicitly identified as Jesus, whom the Jerusalem religious establishment had crucified. They were the guilty party[14]—not the Romans, who carried out the execution, although probably with the complicity of some Jewish leaders.[15] And there is an added claim: only through Jesus can people be saved.

Other New Testament writers also allude to the psalm's architectural metaphor. One of the latest books of the New Testament is a letter attributed to Peter, although almost certainly not written by him but by an anonymous author using his name in the late first century. In it, the author addresses his audience in Asia Minor:

> Come to him, a living stone, rejected by humans but chosen by God, precious; and like living stones let yourselves be built into a spiritual house, as a holy priesthood to offer spiritual sacrifices acceptable to God through Jesus Christ. For scripture has it:
>
>> *"Behold I am placing in Zion a stone*
>>   *a keystone, chosen, precious,*
>> *and whoever believes in it will not be put to shame."*
>
> To you who believe, then, it is precious, but to those who do not believe:
>
>> *"The stone that the builders rejected*
>>   *has become the capstone. . . ."*

But you are a chosen group, a royal priesthood, a holy nation, God's own people, so that you may proclaim the wonderful actions of the one who called you out of darkness into his marvelous light.

For once you were not a people, but now you are the people of God; once you were not shown mercy, but now you have been shown mercy. (1 Peter 2:4–10)

This passage is a collage of quotations from the Jewish scriptures, soon to be called the "Old Testament" or the "Old Covenant" because they were superseded by the "New Testament," the "New Covenant." The main passages quoted are Isaiah 28:16, in which God promises to install a firm foundation in Zion, and Exodus 19:5–6, in which God tells Moses that he will make a covenant with the Israelites and that they will be his "possession more treasured than all peoples . . . a kingdom of priests and a holy nation." To it have been added phrases also originally about Israel, God's "chosen people" (Isaiah 43:20; see also Hosea 2:23).[16] So, in the view of this early Christian writer, the Jews are no longer God's chosen people—Christians are.[17] This is what is called *supersessionism*: Christianity has superseded Judaism. But that was not the view of the earliest Christians, or for that matter of Jesus himself.

The quest for the historical Jesus—who Jesus was (and was not), what he said (and did not say), and what he did (and did not do)— has preoccupied scholars for almost two centuries, ever since most of them came to recognize that the Gospels are not strictly historical accounts. Rather, as their very name, which means "good news," suggests, they are interpretations by different writers with different perspectives of earlier traditions about Jesus, some of which may go back to Jesus himself. The long opening sentence of the Gospel of Luke indicates this:

Since many have attempted to give an orderly account of the events that have been fulfilled among us, just as those who were originally eyewitnesses and servants of the word handed them down to us, it seemed good to me too, having investigated everything carefully from the beginning, to set them in writing systematically for you most excellent Theophilus, so that you may know the certainty about the words that you have received. (Luke 1:1–4)

Here, in a kind of dedication, the anonymous author of this Gospel, traditionally identified as Luke, a minor figure in the New Testament, explains how in his work he intends to set down for fellow believers a reliable account of earlier traditions, both written and oral.[18] Some of those, he says, were based on reports of eyewitnesses, which implicitly he himself was not. Among the earlier accounts Luke has in mind is apparently the Gospel of Mark, which Luke often follows closely, as does Matthew, although both of them correct and supplement Mark. Because of their many similarities, those first three Gospels are called the Synoptic Gospels.

Another reason we have difficulty saying much about the historical Jesus is that the sources that the Gospel writers used included not just earlier traditions about what he said and did, but also the Jewish scriptures. Details of those scriptures—every detail, according to some interpreters—were fulfilled in Jesus, the events of whose life were predicted in them. This is what Luke means by "the events that have been fulfilled among us" in his dedication. He elaborates this belief in a scene near the end of his Gospel. Two days after Jesus had been crucified, two of his disciples were leaving Jerusalem with profound disappointment: they did not know, as we readers do, that he had been raised from the dead. As they were walking along, Jesus mysteriously appeared alongside them and asked them what they were talking about. They expressed surprise that he was unaware of what had happened in Jerusalem:

"About Jesus of Nazareth . . . : How our chief priests and leaders handed him over for the death penalty, and they crucified him. We had hoped that it was he who would set Israel free. . . ." He said to them, "You fools! Your hearts are slow to understand everything that the prophets spoke! Was it not necessary for the Messiah to suffer these things and so enter his glory?" Then, beginning with Moses and the prophets, he interpreted for them the things about himself in all the scriptures. (Luke 24:19–27)

The Jewish scriptures continued to be part of Christian Bibles, but they had been baptized, so to speak: they made sense only when read retrospectively, in the light of Jesus, "about whom Moses in the Law, and the prophets wrote" (John 1:45).[19] Characters such as Isaac, Moses, and David, events such as the Exodus, and institutions such as Passover and the temple are interpreted typologically: they foreshadow Jesus and events in his life. So even an originally simple text such as "the stone that the builders rejected" applies to Jesus.

One thing that is clear from recent scholarship, which has largely broken away from the supersessionism that permeated Christian thought for centuries, is that above all else Jesus was Jewish. Much of what he had to say—as far as we can tell from comparing the four canonical Gospels as well as others—fits nicely into what we know of Jewish thinking during the Roman period in which he lived. Jesus himself and his original followers were all Jews. Jesus did not intend to found a new religion. Rather, he was one in the long line of prophets, seeking to reform Judaism from within. That is what the parable of the vineyard suggests: Jesus is only the most recent of the many messengers God sent to the Israelites.

In the parable of the vineyard only the Jewish leaders are explicitly identified as those responsible for the death of Jesus. Elsewhere in the Synoptic Gospels, however, it is apparently the entire Jewish people who are guilty. According to the Gospel of Matthew, when Pontius Pilate, the Roman governor of Judea, offered to release Jesus in an act of clemency for the Passover, the chief priests and the elders persuaded "the crowds" to ask for Barabbas, probably an insurrectionist, instead.[20] Unable to persuade them, Pilate then sanctimoniously washed his hands, announcing "I am innocent of this man's blood. See to it yourselves!" To this, "all the people" replied: "His blood be on us and on our children" (Matthew 27:24–25). For Matthew, who himself was likely a Jewish Christian, writing after the Romans' destruction of Jerusalem, this self-imprecation may well have applied only to the Jerusalem "crowd"; in another prophecy after the fact, the city's destruction was explained by the guilt of its inhabitants. But Christians have interpreted the self-imprecation as applying not just to Jews living then, but to all Jews ever since.

Although the Synoptic Gospels are ambiguous about collective Jewish guilt for the death of Jesus, the latest Gospel, the Gospel of John, written at the end of the first century, is not. Throughout this Gospel, a distinction is made between Jesus and his Jewish context. In the Synoptic Gospels, Jesus is repeatedly described as teaching in synagogues, as he also is in the Gospel of John.[21] In other places in John, however, there is antagonism between "the synagogue" and Jesus's followers. So, we read that many—including some Jewish leaders—were afraid to admit that they were his followers, "so that they would not be expelled from the synagogue" (12:42).[22] Some scholars think this reflects actual practice in John's community at the end of the first century: Jewish Christians were excommunicated from the synagogues in which they worshipped because of their belief in Jesus. Whether such excommunication ever occurred is debated, but clearly in John boundaries are drawn between Jews and Christians. Moreover, although both Jesus and his followers were Jewish, in John they often seem not to be. In this gospel, Jesus speaks to the Jews of "your law" (8:17; 10:34; see also 15:25), as if it were not also his, and even though Jesus goes to Jerusalem for religious festivals, those festivals are called "the Passover of the Jews" (2:13; 11:53), "the festival of the Jews" (5:1), and "the festival of Tabernacles of the Jews" (7:2), as if Jesus were an outsider. In fact, in the Gospel of John, Jesus himself is called a Jew only once, by a Samaritan woman, herself an outsider (4:9).

I must pause here on the meaning of the term translated "the Jews." The Greek word—*Ioudaioi*—can mean "the Jews," in the sense of adherents to the religion of Judaism. But the terms "Jews" and "Judaism" are originally of geographical origin, meaning persons and the system of beliefs and practices originally from Judah (later Judea); in the New Testament and other literature of the Hellenistic and Roman periods, *Ioudaioi* can mean simply "Judeans," those from Judea as opposed to, for example, Galileans from Galilee and Samaritans from Samaria. In the first century CE, most Judeans were also Jews, but not all Jews were Judeans. The terms are not mutually exclusive, and they overlap. The issue is how to translate the term in the Gospel of John. Some scholars opt for "Judeans," or even "Judean leaders," in a commendable if overly scrupulous attempt to downplay the anti-Semitism both of the Gospel itself and of subsequent Christian history. Others, however, have argued that to remove "Jews" from the New Testament is in effect an anti-Semitic ethnic cleansing. The ambiguity creates problems for translators, but is unavoidable, and may even have been deliberate by the author of the Gospel of John.

In any case, there is anti-Judaism in John's Gospel. In it, the terms "Jew" and "Jews" are used dozens of times, but for the most part to refer to Jesus's opponents, who are repeatedly described as unbelieving despite the miracles—John calls them "signs"—Jesus had performed, and as plotting to kill him. Those Jews who believed in Jesus were "true Israelites" (see John 1:47), while those who did not, whether originally or later, were "from [their] father the devil" (John 8:44). In the end, when Pilate declared that he had found Jesus innocent of any crime, it was "the Jews" who cried out, "Crucify him!" (19:15).

The Gospel of John is the latest of the four Gospels in the New Testament. Although its author was intimately familiar with Judaism, and may himself have experienced some antagonism from non-Christian Jews, the Gospel reflects the increasing separation between Judaism and Christianity. The "Jews" in the Gospel of John are not just those of Jesus's time, but also those of the time when the Gospel was written, when the separation between traditional Jews and Christians, whether Jewish or Gentile, was widening. The Gospel's pejorative view of "the Jews" reflects that separation, rather than being a hostility toward all Jews of all times. Yet that is how it was interpreted soon after and for most of Christian history: Jews were labeled "Christ-killers."

That designation clearly belies history. Not all Jews of Jesus's time were responsible for his death: some were his followers. According to the Gospels, one of those followers, Judas Iscariot, betrayed him to Jewish religious authorities, who in turn handed him over to Pilate for execution on the charge of treason. Undoubtedly some Jews were complicit in Jesus's death, but that hardly justifies the transfer of their guilt to all Jews ever since. Although transgenerational punishment is attributed to God in the Bible, such punishment is clearly unjust, at least for the prophet Ezekiel: "Only the sinner should die. A son should not bear his father's guilt" (Ezekiel 18:20).[23]

Not only is John's Gospel explicitly anti-Semitic in this sense, but it also has a supersessionist high view of Jesus's divinity. For the Gospel's author, despite what the Samaritan woman says to Jesus, salvation comes not from the Jews but only through Jesus, God's son, who reportedly says: "No one comes to the father except through me" (John 14:6).[24] Later Christians will expand this saying to mean "outside the Church there is no salvation": just as only those on Noah's ark were saved during the Flood, none who are not part of the Church will have eternal salvation. By the time Christianity became the official religion of the Roman Empire, both the Jerusalem temple and its successor, a temple to the Roman god Jupiter built by the emperor Hadrian in the early second century CE, lay in ruins—proof of God's divine rejection of both Jews and pagans. Christianity was the true Israel, and the Old Testament was no longer a Jewish book: it was Christian, and only Christians could truly understand it.[25]

What we have then is an increasing—but never total—separation between Judaism and Christianity. The Jewish scriptures became part of the Christian Bible, although they were interpreted in very different ways by the two communities. But as the separation deepened, Christians insisted more and more that they, and only they, were chosen. The Jews had forfeited that status because they had rejected Jesus, God's son, and so the "vineyard" was taken away not just from their leaders, but from all of them, forever.

The prevalence of this attitude throughout Christian history is evident in prayers used by several Christian denominations in their liturgies on Good Friday, the day commemorating Jesus's execution. A series of solemn prayers for that day used in the Roman Catholic Church from the Middle Ages until 1970 includes this:

> Let us also pray for the perfidious Jews: May our Lord and God remove the veil from their hearts, so that they too may acknowledge Jesus Christ, our Lord. Almighty, eternal God, who does not exclude even Jewish perfidy from your mercy, hear our prayers which we offer for the blindness of that people, so that, acknowledging the light of your truth, which is Christ, they may be delivered from their darkness.[26]

The related Latin words translated as "perfidious" and "perfidy" imply treachery and hence the guilt of all Jews for Jesus's death, including the Jewish contemporaries of those making the prayer. Moreover, the prayer (if it is not sacrilegious to call it that), reeks of supersessionism.

The Greek Orthodox liturgy for Holy Friday, still in use, is similar in tone. Here is just a sample:

> Thus says the Lord to the Jews: "My people, what have I done to you, and how have you repaid me? Instead of manna, gall; instead of water, vinegar; instead of loving me, you nail me to the cross. I can bear no more. I shall call the Gentiles mine. They will glorify Me with the Father and the Spirit, and I shall give them life eternal."[27]

The Anglican Church shared these sentiments. Its essentially official liturgical text for many centuries, the 1662 edition of *The Book of Common Prayer* includes this Good Friday prayer:

> O merciful God, who hast made all men, and hatest nothing that thou hast made, nor desirest the death of a sinner, but rather that he should be converted and live: Have mercy upon all Jews, Turks, Infidels, and Heretics, and take from them all ignorance, hardness of heart, and contempt of thy Word; and so fetch them

home, blessed Lord, to thy flock, that they may be saved among the remnant of the true Israelites, and be made one fold under one shepherd, Jesus Christ our Lord.[28]

In modern times, church authorities have softened the offensive tone of some of these prayers. The latest version (1979) of *The Book of Common Prayer* used in the United States simply omits the prayer immediately above. The 2011 revision of the Roman Catholic liturgy for Good Friday has this version of the earlier prayer:

> Let us pray also for the Jewish people, to whom the Lord our God spoke first, that he may grant them to advance in love of his name and in faithfulness to his covenant. Almighty ever-living God, who bestowed your promises on Abraham and his descendants, hear graciously the prayers of your Church, that the people you first made your own may attain the fullness of redemption.[29]

This revised prayer is very close to Paul's view that the Jews were still God's chosen people, but it conveniently glosses over the long history of Christian supersessionism, including Christians' self-designation as the new chosen people, usually meaning the loss of this status for Jews. It also ignores the long history of anti-Semitism, a history that begins in the New Testament and has been a horrifying constant in Christian history ever since, the "dark shadow" that follows Christianity through time.[30]

7

BEYOND THE BIBLE

Sacred Texts and Sacred Places

BECAUSE THE BIBLE is an anthology of works written by human beings over many hundreds of years, we should read it not as divine revelation, not as God's word about God, but rather as what different writers thought about God and how they projected onto God their own views, especially to enhance the status of the groups to which they belonged. With its multiple layers, the Bible allows and even invites us to read it in this way. Indeed, some biblical writers make it clear that the choice of an heir or a king or a group was personal or political rather than divine. Thus, we do not need to think of Abraham's family, or some subset of it, or some subset of a subset, as divinely chosen. This understanding also acquits the biblical god of partiality and of repeated acts of violence, all projected onto him by human writers. Those not chosen do not have a divinely imposed inferiority, nor did God command that they be enslaved or slaughtered.

Eventually, however, some ancient Israelite writings acquired a special status. Human texts became sacred texts, now shaping and guiding the communities that accepted them as divine revelation about what they should believe and how they should act. This process begins in the later biblical period, for example, when in the fourth century BCE, the book of Chronicles combines Leviticus and Jeremiah in order to explain the Judeans' exile in Babylonia. It can also have severe consequences, as when in the mid-fifth century BCE, Nehemiah quotes the by-then authoritative book of Deuteronomy as support for dissolving mixed marriages. As the Bible came to be thought of as eternally true and relevant to every new context, biblical texts were often used to justify one group's prejudice against others, such as the exiles returned from Babylonia's ostracizing of "the people of the land" and Christians' blaming Jews for having crucified Jesus.

Christians mined the Jewish scriptures for revelation about themselves and their executed leader, appropriating not just the language of chosenness, but also many elements of Jewish belief and practice. Christians in effect say to Jews: "All that you have is true—your god is our god, your scriptures are part of our scriptures—but you have missed the final and definitive revelation made by that god in Jesus of Nazareth." Jesus is identified as the new Passover lamb, with his death described as fulfilling the requirements of the ancient Israelite ritual commemorating the Exodus from Egypt.[1] Christian Baptism is like a personal Exodus, a passage through water from slavery to sin to new life in Christ.[2] The "old covenant" of Mount Sinai has been revoked, and transferred to believers in Jesus.

Another group that mined the Jewish sacred texts—and Christian sacred texts as well—was the early Muslim community. The notion that Muslims are specially chosen by God is not explicitly stated in Islam's sacred text, the Qur'an, perhaps because Islam's primary focus is on acceptance of God's revelation in the Qur'an rather than divine choice of one tribal or ethnic group. But the Qur'an draws on both Jewish and Christian traditions, just as the New Testament draws on the Jewish scriptures. In the pages of the Qur'an we find repeated references to such familiar characters as Ishmael and Isaac, Moses and Aaron, David and Solomon, and John the Baptist, Mary, and Jesus. Muslims in effect say to Jews and Christians, both of whom the Qur'an calls "the people of the Book": "Your god is our god,[3] your scriptures are part of our scripture[4]—but you both have missed the final revelation made by your god and our god to Muhammad, the last and greatest of the prophets."[5] So, the Muslim community broadly speaking often thinks of itself as superior to Jews and Christians, just as Christians often do to Jews, and for that matter, as Jews often do to Christians and Muslims.

Judaism, Christianity, and Islam are frequently called the Abrahamic religions. Jews trace their genealogy back to Abraham, through Jacob and Isaac; as a Jew, Jesus was thus also a descendant of Abraham, as genealogies in the Gospels record.[6] For Christians more generally, Abraham is a model believer.[7] In the Qur'an, Abraham is the biblical character most frequently mentioned—some sixty-nine times. Muslims see themselves as connected to Abraham (in Arabic, *Ibrahim*) through Ishmael, Abraham's son with Hagar and the ancestor of Arabian tribes, including that of the prophet Muhammad. For Muslims more generally, Abraham is also a model believer, a pure monotheist, in fact, the first *muslim*, which literally means "one who surrenders [to God]." According to the Qur'an, "Abraham was neither a Jew nor a Christian, but a man of pristine faith, a Muslim, nor was he an idolater" (3:68).[8]

The complex interrelationship of the three Abrahamic religions is not just textual, however; it is also spatial, as the history of a prominent sacred place in Jerusalem illustrates. In the southeast corner of the Old City of Jerusalem is a massive elevated platform known to Jews as the Temple Mount and to Muslims as Haram esh-Sharif ("The Noble Sanctuary"). Originally a threshing area just north of the town the Israelites had captured early in David's reign, David purchased it as the site for an altar to Yahweh, and his son and successor Solomon built the First Temple there in the tenth century BCE.[9] This was the temple that the Babylonians and Edomites destroyed in 586 BCE. Its successor, the Second Temple, was built in the late sixth century BCE by returned exiles from Babylonia. That complex was completely rebuilt by King Herod the Great in the late first century BCE; this was the temple in which Jesus preached and worshipped, and which the Romans destroyed in 70 CE during the First Jewish Revolt. All that remained were the retaining walls of the platform, whose "Western Wall" has been a place of Jewish prayer and pilgrimage since the Middle Ages. Jerusalem has thus been "the holy city" for Judaism both for the more than one thousand years the temple was in existence and for the nearly two thousand years since.[10]

In Jewish tradition as early as the books of Chronicles, the site of the temple was further identified as Mount Moriah, where Genesis says Abraham was prepared to sacrifice his son Isaac in obedience to God's command.[11] At the time, however, according to Genesis, Abraham was in the far south, in the vicinity of Beer-sheba, so it is likely that the name *Moriah* was transferred from the Beer-sheba region in order to connect the site of the temple with Abraham, just as Muslim tradition would relocate Moriah (in Arabic, *Marwah*) to Mecca.[12]

One corollary of Christians' self-designation as the new chosen people, replacing the Jews, was that as the Roman Empire became Christian in the fourth century CE, Christians claimed the Promised Land as their own. Because it was where Jesus's life, death, and burial had taken place, it now became the "holy land" for Christians, and for them, too, Jerusalem was the "holy city."[13] Sacred places associated especially with Jesus and with other biblical characters and events became pilgrimage sites. Churches were built all over the region, often on the sites of synagogues and temples to Greek and Roman gods, and monasteries and convents dotted the landscape. In 325, Constantine ordered the destruction of the temple of Jupiter in Jerusalem, built in the early 130s on the Temple Mount over the ruins of the Second Temple. Soon thereafter, the most important Christian shrine, the Church of the Holy Sepulcher, also known as the Church of the Resurrection (in Greek, *Anastasis*), was built on the probably correctly identified site of Jesus's tomb now inside the Old City.

For Muslims, Jerusalem is also a holy city, as shown in its Arabic name, Al-Quds ("the holy"). According to the Qur'an, one night God transported Muhammad from the Holy Mosque in Mecca to what the Qur'an calls "the farthest [in Arabic, *al-aqsa*] mosque" (17:1), originally probably meaning the entire Temple Mount. The mosque built on the south side of the Haram esh-Sharif in the late seventh century was therefore called Al-Aqsa, as were its successors. Later Muslim traditions elaborate on this verse, describing how the prophet was transported from Mecca to Jerusalem on the great white stallion

Buraq, whose name means "lightning." After tethering his mount to the Western Wall, he was taken from a rock on the Temple Mount up into heaven, where he met with Abraham, Moses, Jesus, and other prophets, and finally with God himself. The rock is almost certainly the original threshing floor that David had purchased. An indentation in the rock's surface is identified as the footprint left by Muhammad as he ascended to heaven for his visit with God.[14] It is now within the magnificent Dome of the Rock on the Haram esh-Sharif which, dating to 691 CE, is the oldest surviving monument of Islamic architecture. Its gold dome and its colorful glazed tiles, many decorated with calligraphic quotations from the Qur'an, have made it the visual focal point of Jerusalem. Because of these connections, Jerusalem is the third holiest city for Muslims, after Mecca and Medina.

Christian control of the Holy Land was brief, lasting only three centuries. Muslims took over Jerusalem in 638 CE, and the new rulers were generally tolerant of both Jews and Christians. In the early eleventh century, however, Caliph al-Hakim ordered the destruction of the Church of the Holy Sepulcher, and Jews as well as Christians were persecuted for a time throughout the Holy Land. A briefer period of Christian control of the Holy Land occurred from the late eleventh to the late thirteenth centuries during the Crusades, whose religious motivation was to rescue the Christian holy places from infidel Muslim rule. The Crusaders misidentified the Al-Aqsa mosque as Solomon's palace, making it their own seat of government, and repurposed the Dome of the Rock as a church. When in 1291 the Crusaders lost their last stronghold, the city of Acre on the Mediterranean coast, total Muslim control of the Holy Land resumed and both the Al-Aqsa mosque and the Dome of the Rock became Muslim holy places again. After the defeat of the Ottoman Empire in World War I, Palestine became a British mandate, but the new rulers did not change the status of the holy places of the Abrahamic religions, especially in the Old City of Jerusalem. After the Israeli–Arab war of 1948, the Old City came under Jordanian control; Jews there were forced to flee and they had no access to the Western Wall and the Temple Mount until the 1967 war, when Israel captured the Old City.

So, all three faiths consider the same places sacred, because of their actual or imagined connections with Jewish, Christian, and Muslim leaders and events as found in their respective scriptures. Those scriptures—the Hebrew Bible/Old Testament, the New Testament, and the Qur'an—have been and continue to be used to support sometimes overlapping, sometimes competing claims of the three faiths to Jerusalem's holiest sites.

Sometimes, too, Jewish, Christian, and Muslim extremists have used violence in these places to enhance their own claims and to subvert those of others. In 1969, Denis Michael Rohan, a fundamentalist Christian, attempted to set fire to the Al-Aqsa mosque, hoping that its destruction would allow the rebuilding of the Jewish temple and hasten the Second Coming of Christ; when I visited the Haram esh-Sharif the following year, charred timbers still littered its southern part. In 1982, Alan Goodman, an ultrareligious American-Israeli nationalist, took an assault rifle inside the Dome of the Rock and opened fire, killing two and wounding several more. At moments of political tension, Palestinian young men have hurled down stones from the Haram esh-Sharif onto Jewish worshippers at the Western Wall below; as a result, frequently only Palestinian men older than forty-five have been allowed to enter the Haram on Friday, the Muslim holy day. Attacks like these on places of worship and on worshippers themselves are desecrations contrary to two fundamental principles of all three Abrahamic religions, love of God and love of neighbor.[15]

∎ ∎ ∎

IN THE CHAPTERS THAT FOLLOW, I will focus on specific examples of modern Christian and Jewish groups who appropriated the status of chosen people for themselves, interpreting the words of the Bible as actually about them and thereby legitimating their politics and their territorial claims then and now.[16] Finally, I will consider both positive and negative aspects of biblical views on the contemporary issues of immigrants and refugees in light of the concept of chosenness.

8

GOD SHED HIS
LIGHT ON THEE?

IN THE EARLY SIXTEENTH CENTURY, English Puritans began to colonize what they eventually called "New England." Financial gain and imperial expansion had been the main objectives of earlier colonizers of the Western Hemisphere, including not only the Spanish, the Portuguese, the French, and the Dutch, but also the first English settlers of Virginia. Some also had a religious motive—to convert the original inhabitants of those lands to Christianity—but missionary activity was largely secondary. For the Puritans who settled in New England, however, the motivation was reversed. Although commercial activity may have been part of their objective, or at least an objective of the Crown that had given them charters, for most Puritans a religious motive was primary. The Puritans were dissidents; in their view, the Church of England had not reformed sufficiently. Many had been forced to flee from England to continental Europe for their beliefs, and now they intended to establish in the "New World" a commonwealth where they could worship freely. Their self-identification as God's new Israel has had a profound and enduring influence on American politics and political discourse.[1]

The first Puritans to reach New England did so on the *Mayflower*, eventually settling at Plymouth, Massachusetts, in 1620. They had made a "covenant" to establish a social order in their colony. One of them, William Bradford, elected several times as governor of the colony, later penned his reminiscences in *Of Plymouth Plantation*.[2] In this combination memoir and exhortation, he wrote: "May not and ought not the children of these fathers rightly say: *Our fathers were Englishmen which came over this great ocean, and were ready to perish in this wilderness; but they cried unto the Lord, and he heard their voice, and looked on their adversity, etc.*"[3] The italicized words above (as in the original publication) are quotations from the Bible, and their sources are given in Bradford's notes. But here is what the Bible says, in the Geneva Bible, the preferred translation of the Puritans: "A Syrian was my father, who being ready to perish for hunger, went down into Egypt. . . . And the Egyptians vexed us, and troubled us, and laded us with cruel bondage. But when we cried unto the Lord God of our fathers, the Lord heard our voice, and looked on our adversity, and on our labor, and on our oppression" (Deuteronomy 26:5–7). The verses are from the book of Deuteronomy, which presents itself as Moses's final address to the Israelites as they are poised to cross the Jordan River and enter the Promised Land of Canaan. Bradford's quotation is only partially accurate—perhaps it is from memory. But the text is also strategically changed: "my father" has become "our fathers," and "Englishmen" has been added as though it were part of the original text, although every learned divine would know that it was not. The altered quotation clearly shows how for the Puritans the Bible was not just a record of what had happened and what had been revealed to the ancient Israelites and earliest Christians, but a living text whose underlying viewpoint and even words were easily transferable to the Puritans themselves.

From their earliest days, then, the English Puritan colonists of New England viewed themselves as a new chosen people. For them the Jewish scriptures contained a prophetic typology of their own history, just as it had for the early Christians. Like Moses, Bradford led the Puritans, escaping oppression, across the ocean to a new Promised Land, a "Providence plantation" in the wilderness of "new Canaan," where they made a new covenant with God and with each other.[4]

The next wave of Puritans was prompted by persecution in England during the reign of King Charles I, which in their view paralleled the pharaoh's persecution of the Israelites in Egypt. As several hundred of them were preparing to set sail from Southampton, England, in 1630, they were preached to by John Cotton, himself a Puritan but not as fiercely dissident as those in his audience.[5] In the sermon, titled "God's Promise to His Plantation," Cotton took as his text "I will appoint a place for my people Israel, and I will plant them, that they may dwell in a place of their own, and move no more" (2 Samuel 7:10). Cotton maintains that "the placing of a people in this or that country is from the appointment of the Lord,"[6] and that the Puritan colonization of Massachusetts proceeds upon a "warrant out of the word of God."[7] Cotton's view of the Bible as a divinely inspired text that speaks directly to the present is similar to Bradford's. In Cotton's theology, God's word will never fail to be fulfilled, a guarantee that this new divinely ordained plantation will prosper and flourish.[8]

This understanding of the Puritan settlement as already promised in the Bible is geographically illustrated in the map of New England, whose landscape is dotted with names of biblical places: Canaan, Bethlehem, Zion, Salem, Jericho, Jordan River, Mount Carmel, and many more. With the westward expansion of the United States, the same use of biblical place names spread to other regions.[9]

For Thomas Hooker, who arrived in Massachusetts in 1633, the Babylonian exile of the sixth century BCE provided another parallel to the Puritans' own experience. In his farewell sermon, preached immediately before his departure, he announced: "God is going, his glory is departing, England hath seen her best days, and now evil days are befalling us: God is packing up his Gospel, because nobody will buy his wares, nor come to his price."[10] Just as in the prophet Ezekiel's vision, Yahweh's glory had left Jerusalem to be with the exiles in Babylonia, so now God was leaving "Old England."[11] Similarly, in 1639, Richard Mather, another recent arrival, wrote discussing Jeremiah 50:5, "Come, and let us join ourselves to the Lord in a perpetual covenant that shall not be forgotten" (King James Version):

> Although that which is foretold . . . in the fourth and fifth verses of this chapter, was in part fulfilled when the people of God returned from captivity in Babylon at the end of seventy years: yet

we must not limit the place to that time only, but may extend
it further . . . : so many things that literally concerned the Jews
were types and figures, signifying the like things concerning the
people of God in these latter days.[12]

There is a gentle, if naïve, tone to all this. God has a plan, revealed
in scripture. The Puritans' emigration is part of that plan, and their
faith should give them confidence.

Either before or during their voyage in 1630, the Puritans heard
another sermon, given by John Winthrop, their elected governor.[13]
Called "A Model of Christian Charity," it exhorted those about to
cross the Atlantic to follow biblical teaching by practicing both justice and mercy in their dealings with each other. Much of the sermon
is unremarkable in its blandness, and its style and language are highly
biblical, echoing Moses's farewell address to the Israelites in the book
of Deuteronomy. Perhaps even then, Winthrop, like Bradford before
him, was thought of—and thought of himself—as a new Moses. In
his conclusion, Winthrop interpolates references to the Puritans
themselves into an adapted text of Deuteronomy 30:15–20.[14] Just as
God's continuing protection of the ancient Israelites was conditional
upon their obeying the terms of his covenant with them, so, too, the
Puritans had to keep their covenant with God, or else they would
perish in this new Promised Land. Clearly, Winthrop identified the
ancient Israelites as a prototype of the Puritans, who had a similar
choice presented to them.

Near the end of the sermon, Winthrop reminds his audience of
biblical examples of those who had failed to observe divinely given
commands. If they do not "follow the counsel of Micah, 'to do justly,
to love mercy, to walk humbly with our God'" (Micah 6:8), then they,
too, will suffer divine wrath. But if they do live as the prophet ad-
vised, then they will be a model for the rest of the world and for future
generations: "For we should consider that we shall be as a city upon a
hill. The eyes of all people are upon us."[15]

Winthrop's phrase "a city upon a hill" alludes to Jesus's words to
his followers in the Sermon on the Mount:

You are the light of the world. A city set on a hill cannot be hidden. Nor does anyone light a lamp and then put it under a bushel basket, but on the lampstand, and it gives light to all in the house. So let your light shine before people, so that they may see your good works and give glory to your father who is in heaven. (Matthew 5:14–16)

For Winthrop, as originally for Jesus (or at least for Matthew), the metaphor of a city on a hill was not a statement of fact—not simply a "you are special," as it were. Rather, it was a moral exhortation: because of your special status you should live exemplary lives. But what started as a moral exhortation became triumphalist and virtually canonical as it reverberated through American history.

For the Puritans, the conviction that they were the new Israel was fraught with responsibility and risk. If they failed to observe God's laws, then he would punish them, just as he had repeatedly punished biblical Israel. So, in a sermon on election day—an annual holiday in each New England colony and state from the seventeenth to the early nineteenth centuries—in Hartford, May 14, 1685, Samuel Wakeman took as his text "Be thou instructed, O Jerusalem" (Jeremiah 6:8), and proclaimed:

Jerusalem was, New England is, they were, you are God's own, God's Covenant People, and what concerned them in that their day, no less concerns you in this your day, this word . . . to Jacob . . . comes now to be applied to you; change but the persons and the relation is the same . . . : put but in New England's name instead of that of Jerusalem, and to you belongs, to you is the word of the solemn caution and admonition sent.[16]

But this nuanced view of divine choice soon morphed into one less so. A century later, Ezra Stiles, the president of Yale College, preached a sermon titled "The United States Elevated to Glory and Honor," also on the occasion of the election of the governor and other Connecticut officials, shortly after the ceasefire between Britain and the colonies in April 1783. The sermon, which lasted nearly two hours, is a lengthy elaboration of the proposition that the United States had been specially divinely chosen. Stiles took as his text a verse from Deuteronomy: "And to make thee high above all nations, which he hath made, in praise, and in name, and in honor; and that thou mayest be an holy people unto the Lord thy God" (Deuteronomy 26:19 [King James Version]). Stiles was an educated Christian minster, well versed in the Bible and fluent in Hebrew and Greek. He knew that in their original context these words had been addressed by Moses to the Israelites near the end of his life at the base of Mount Nebo. But Stiles was also a millenarian, and believed that these words, like all scripture, were a form of prophecy, to be finally fulfilled only at the Second Coming of Christ and after his thousand-year reign. At that time,[17] he thought, three events predicted in biblical prophecy would simultaneously occur: "The annihilation of the pontificate, the reassembling of the Jews, and the fullness of the gentiles."[18] Roman Catholicism would cease to exist and the Jews would not only be returned to their Promised Land, but they would convert to Christianity, recognizing Christ as the prince of peace and thus becoming the people that Moses had supposedly foreseen.

For Stiles, the new United States had a special role in preparing for this event. Again, Moses's words to the Israelites ultimately refer to the United States:

> God hath still greater blessings in store, for this vine which his own right hand hath planted,[19] to make . . . his American Israel, *high above all nations which he hath made,* in numbers, *and in praise, and in name, and in honor!*[20]

In Stiles's political typology, George Washington is the "American Joshua . . . raised up by God," a "man of God, greatly beloved of the Most High," for our independence was "sealed and confirmed by God in the victory of General Washington at Trenton."[21] God was also apparently directly responsible for the discovery of Benedict Arnold's treason, for the arrival of the French fleet at Yorktown, and for other details of the American Revolution, now one of the "wars of the Lord."[22] Stiles's exuberant optimism in the afterglow of the victory over the British was shared by John Adams, whom he quotes: "But the great designs of providence must be accomplished;—great indeed! . . . Light spreads from the day-spring in the west; and may it shine more and more until the perfect day."[23]

What had started as a nuanced spiritual conviction by this time was becoming American "civil religion,"[24] with its canonical texts—the Declaration of Independence and the Constitution; its places of pilgrimage—Boston, Philadelphia, Valley Forge, Washington, DC; its relics—the Minuteman Trail, the Liberty Bell, the flag; and its quasi-holy days and rituals. But this "civil religion" was not really secular: its roots were in the Bible. Benjamin Franklin's never-realized 1776 design for the Great Seal of the United States depicted, in his own words:

> Moses standing on the Shore, and extending his Hand over the Sea, thereby causing the same to overwhelm Pharaoh who is sitting in an open Chariot, a Crown on his Head and a Sword in his Hand. Rays from a Pillar of Fire in the Clouds reaching to Moses, to express that he acts by Command of the Deity.[25]

Surrounding this scene is the motto "Rebellion to tyrants is obedience to God." The symbolism is transparent: the tyrant is King George III, "the sullen-tempered Pharaoh of England," as Thomas Paine called him in *Common Sense* that same year.[26] Those who escaped his tyranny are, like the Israelites leaving Egypt, specially favored by God.

The Continental Congress did not like Franklin's design. Instead, it eventually adopted in 1782 the images now familiar because of their use on the back of the one-dollar bill. The obverse depicts the eye of Providence in a triangle (representing the Trinity) under the thirteen-letter Latin motto *Annuit coeptis*, "He (God) has nodded in approval of (our) beginnings," words loosely borrowed from the Roman poet Virgil's *Aeneid* (9.625). The triangle forms the apex of a pyramid of thirteen steps (for the original thirteen states), symbolizing strength and duration, according to Charles Thomson, the seal's designer. Under the pyramid is the motto *Novus ordo seclorum*, "a new order of the ages," a phrase adapted from lines in Virgil's *Eclogues* (4.5–8) often interpreted by Christians as predicting the birth of Christ. So, the seal expresses the belief that the Christian God has personally approved of this new and implicitly permanent enterprise, no less momentous than the coming of the Messiah.

In the nineteenth century, America's self-understanding as the new chosen people became even more immodest. In 1845, the journalist John O'Sullivan asserted that America had a "manifest destiny to overspread the continent allotted by Providence" and to annex the Republic of Texas and the Oregon Territory.[27] A few years later, Herman Melville, in a lengthy authorial aside in his novel *White Jacket*, declared:

> We Americans are the peculiar, chosen people—the Israel of our time; we bear the ark of the liberties of the world. . . . We are the pioneers of the world; the advance-guard, sent on through the wilderness of untried things, to break a new path in the New World that is ours.[28]

Not long after Melville had written these words, *Harper's New Monthly Magazine* published in 1858 a lengthy unsigned editorial called "Providence in American History." Its author expressed the conviction that "Providence has presided over the colonization and progress of this country . . . and will fulfill its far-reaching scheme." He goes on to say of "our continent":

> Taken in whole, it is a wonderful provision for the intelligence, sagacity, energy, restlessness, and indomitable will of such a race as the Anglo-Saxon—a race that masters physical nature without being mastered by it—a race in which the intensest home-feelings combine with a love of enterprise, adventure, and colonization—a race that fears nothing, claims every thing within reach, enjoys the future more than the present, and believes in a destiny

of incomparable and immeasurable grandeur. Without the least extravagance it may be said that there never was such a charac-ter—such elements of activity, foresight, sovereignty—acting on a theatre so broad, so ample, so wonderful. . . . True now as true of old in Horeb: "Put off thy shoes from off thy feet; for the place whereon thou standest is holy ground."[29]

The final quotation is God's instruction to Moses from the burning bush at Mount Horeb, repeated almost verbatim to Joshua once the Israelites had entered Canaan.[30] The writer conceives of the United States as the new Promised Land and its Constitution as an inspired text on a par with the Bible itself.

In the index to the magazine, the editorial's author is listed as A. A. Lipscomb, who was a frequent contributor to "Editor's Table," the regular column in which this essay appeared. Lipscomb was a min-ister and educator, who a dozen years earlier had written *Our Coun-try: Its Danger and Duty*, a pamphlet in which he "fearlessly exposed" "the baleful superstitions" of "Popery . . . the Antichrist of the Bible," which threatened the "pure Christianity" which is "the religion of our country."[31] Lipscomb's editorial appeared at a time when many Irish Catholics had started to immigrate to the United States because of the "Great Famine" caused by a blight on potatoes; the arrival of these "Papists" was apparently a reason for Anglo-Saxon concern.

The arrogance of American exceptionalism on display here is breathtaking. It would lead to nativism, prejudice against anyone considered "other." For exceptionalists, those not chosen have in-cluded, at various times, Native Americans, African Americans, Irish Americans, German Americans, Italian Americans, Asian Ameri-cans, Latino/as, Roman Catholics, Lutherans, and Jews, among many others. So, as in ancient Israel at various periods, not all are chosen—only those who agree with, and look like, the people who designate themselves as chosen.

By the end of the nineteenth century, America's self-appointed, self-anointed mission provided justification for imperial expansion beyond the North American continent. During Albert J. Beveridge's successful campaign in 1898 for a US Senate seat in Indiana, in a speech titled "The March of the Flag," he justifies the "resistless march" of the American people "toward the commercial supremacy of the world,"[32] and cavalierly disposes of the issue of the right of conquered peoples to self-government by labeling them as unenlightened and incapable of ruling themselves. He concludes by again likening Americans to the divinely led Israelites escaping from Egypt:

> Fellow-Americans, we are God's chosen people. . . . His great purposes are revealed in the progress of the flag, which . . . leads us, like a holier pillar of cloud by day and pillar of fire by night, into situations unforeseen by finite wisdom and duties unexpected by the unprophetic heart of selfishness. . . . We cannot retreat from any soil where Providence has unfurled our banner; it is ours to save that soil for Liberty and Civilization.[33]

Beveridge's self-righteousness echoes throughout American political discourse to the present. American exceptionalism has become a dogma recited by politicians of all persuasions. Since 1954, we have pledged that we are "one nation under God," echoing the Puritans' self-identification as God's new Israel and the special status that implied. Ronald Reagan established the practice of having presidential speeches end by invoking God's blessing on America.[34] What had been for Jesus—and for Winthrop—a metaphorical city on a hill, became for Reagan and too many others the "shining city" that is the United States.[35] On the first anniversary of the attacks on September 11, 2001, when George W. Bush spoke of "the ideal of America" as "the light" that "shines in the darkness," he was not just riffing on the metaphor of the city on a hill.[36] Rather, he was echoing words referring to Jesus himself (John 1:4–5), and at least implicitly identifying the United States as the Messiah.[37] In another age this might be called blasphemy; now it is simply part of the American myth, itself based on much older myths.

But dressing up American exceptionalism in biblical language does not make it true. Roger Williams, the dissident who left the dissidents of Plymouth Colony for Rhode Island in 1636, later wrote to John Winthrop's son that thinking of the Puritan commonwealth as "God Land" was a kind of deification akin to idolatry: "God Land will be (as it now is) as great a God with us English as God Gold was with the Spaniards."[38] Perhaps we should return to the modesty of Abraham Lincoln, who shortly before his first inauguration as president characterized the United States as the Almighty's "almost chosen people."[39]

9

FUNDAMENTALIST ZIONISMS

HISTORY CASTS DOUBT on the belief that God's choice of the Jewish people as his "treasured possession" meant that the land of Canaan was to be theirs forever. In biblical times alone, Jerusalem, their sacred capital that God had supposedly sworn to protect, was twice destroyed by foreign armies—the Babylonians in 586 BCE and the Romans in 70 CE. Moreover, their sovereignty over Canaan was partial and brief, lasting only a few centuries in the several thousand years from when the land was first reportedly promised to Abraham until the mid-twentieth century. Finally, most Jews were scattered, first in the Middle East, and eventually throughout the world, although some continued to live in Jerusalem and Palestine under Babylonian, Persian, Greek, Roman, Christian, Muslim, Crusader, Turkish, and eventually British rule. God had apparently not given the land of Canaan to the Jews, since for most of their history they had not controlled it.

Still, Jewish attachment to the land persevered. "Next year in Jerusalem" became a refrain repeated every Passover, wherever it was celebrated, in Damascus or Cairo, Rome or Grenada, Berlin or London, New York, Buenos Aires, or Beijing. Until the late nineteenth century, however, that wish was unfulfilled for almost all Jews. Then, motivated by anti-Semitism throughout Europe, Theodor Herzl organized the First Zionist Congress, which met in Basel, Switzerland, in 1897. Herzl's goal was essentially political: because Jews were unable to achieve anything approaching safety, let alone equality, in Europe, their best recourse was to have their own national state. This aspiration paralleled those of other groups in an era of self-determination, especially Italy under Garibaldi in 1870 and Germany under Bismarck in 1871. The obvious place for such a state was the ancient Promised Land, in Herzl's time that part of the Ottoman Empire known as Palestine. The Nazi Holocaust tragically proved the wisdom of Herzl's plan, as would the persecution and expulsion of Jews from Arab countries after the founding of the state of Israel in 1948.

The Jewish population of Palestine from 70 CE to 1948 was minute compared to those living outside the Promised Land, in the Diaspora. After the Second Jewish Revolt against the Romans in 132–35 CE, Jews were essentially barred from entering Jerusalem, a prohibition that continued when Christianity became the official religion of the Roman Empire in the late fourth century. Under Muslim (first Arab, then Ottoman) rule, however, beginning in the seventh century and continuing to the early twentieth, Jews and Christians usually had the status of quasi-protected minorities. The approximate population of Palestine at the end of the nineteenth century was about 500,000, of whom about 12 percent were Christians and 8 percent Jews. The Zionist movement motivated many European Jews to immigrate to Palestine, both before and after World War I, as well as immediately after World War II. Although still a minority, the Jewish proportion of the population increased, as shown in the following table, based on rough approximations:

	TOTAL POPULATION	MUSLIMS	JEWS	CHRISTIANS (BOTH ARAB AND NON-ARAB)
1890	500,000	400,000 (80%)	40,000 (8%)	60,000 (12%)
1914	700,000	525,000 (75%)	98,000 (14%)	71,000 (11%)
1931	1,000,000	735,000 (74%)	170,000 (17%)	86,000 (9%)
1947	2,000,000	1,200,000 (60%)	640,000 (32%)	160,000 (8%)[1]

In what follows, I discuss ultrareligious Zionism, both Jewish and Christian. I do not intend to discuss the larger historical issues associated with Zionism and the establishment of the modern state of Israel, such as whether or not it is a form of European colonialism. My own view is that history cannot be undone and that the rights of all residents of Israel and Palestine need to be respected and protected. Here, as elsewhere in this book, I focus on how various groups selectively use the Bible to support claims of special status. Put simply, ultrareligious Zionists, both Jewish and Christian, believe that because the Bible says God promised the land of Canaan to the Israelites, then it belongs to their descendants, the chosen people, the Jews, in perpetuity.

Herzl's goal was the establishment of a Jewish state, not the restoration of Israel in fulfillment of biblical promises. When the Ottoman sultan refused to allow such a state in Palestine, Herzl toyed with the idea of establishing it at least temporarily in British East Africa (now Uganda), which indicates that, for him, Zionism was political and secular. Religious Zionism was significantly different. One of its most important proponents was Rabbi Avraham Yitzhak Kook (1865–1935), who had immigrated from what is now Latvia to Palestine in 1904, and who became chief Ashkenazi rabbi of Palestine in 1921. He saw the settlement of Palestine by Jews as the beginning of the process of the redemption of the world, a process that would culminate in the coming of the Messiah and the conversion of all nations to Judaism as foretold by biblical prophecies. The idea of redemption made its way into the Declaration of the Establishment of the State of Israel (1948), the Israeli equivalent of the American Declaration of Independence. Near its end, this founding document speaks of "the great struggle for the realization of the age-old dream—the redemption of Israel,"[2] an ambiguous nod in the direction of the religious Zionists.[3]

Kook's ideas and those of his son, Rabbi Zvi Yehuda Kook (1891–1982), became the ideological support for the ultrareligious Zionist movement after the Arab–Israeli wars of 1967 and 1973, in which Israel captured the West Bank (including the Old City of Jerusalem) from Jordan, the Golan Heights from Syria, and the Gaza Strip and Sinai Peninsula from Egypt. The growth of movements such as Gush Emunim ("the bloc of the faithful"), now known as Ne'emanei Eretz Yisrael ("those faithful to the land of Israel"), in effect constituted a kind of religious Zionist revival.[4] In their view, Jews were to reclaim the ancient

Jewish homelands by establishing settlements in all the captured—or, as they called them, "liberated"—territories. One slogan of such groups is "Eretz Yisrael Hashlemah," often translated "Greater Israel," but which literally means "the entire (or complete) land of Israel." For ultrareligious Zionists, who are a minority in the Jewish community worldwide, "the land of Israel" includes at a minimum all the territory west of the Jordan River, under the acronym "Yesha," which stands for Judah (in Hebrew, *Yehudah*), Samaria (*Shomron*), and Gaza ('*Aza*). Not long after the 1967 war, the younger Rabbi Kook insisted:

> I tell you explicitly that the Torah forbids us to surrender even one inch of our liberated land. There are no conquests here and we are not occupying foreign lands; we are returning to our home, to the inheritance of our ancestors. There is no Arab land here, only the inheritance of our God—and the more the world gets used to this thought the better it will be for them and for all of us.[5]

A claim to Samaria, at least, is biblically problematic, since in the view of some biblical writers, those who lived there after its conquest by the Assyrians in 722 BCE were idolaters; only the kingdom of Judah was truly chosen.[6]

But ultrareligious Zionists did not limit Israel's supposedly divinely given territory to pre-1967 Israel and the territories captured in 1967 and 1973. According to Gush Emunim, Lebanon was also "part of the heritage of our ancestors, the tribes of Asher, Naphtali, and Zebulun."[7] Some extremists have even taken literally the boundaries of the land promised to Abraham in Genesis—"from the river of Egypt to the great river, the River Euphrates" (Genesis 15:18)—that is, all the land from Egypt to northern Syria, including the modern kingdom of Jordan.[8] After all, the first Zionist was God, not Herzl, asserted Moshe Levinger, a student of the younger Rabbi Kook and an ultrareligious settler activist.[9]

The choice of proof texts for these claims is selective. Although the repeated promise of the land to Abraham in Genesis is unconditional, other biblical passages speak of the possession of the land as conditional upon the Israelites' obeying divinely revealed laws: failure to do so would result in conquest of the land by foreign powers and the exile of its inhabitants. Finally, different biblical writers give different boundaries for the land promised.[10]

In recent decades, religious Zionism has both grown and become more fundamentalist in Israel. Its adherents have been largely responsible for the rapid growth of settlements in the West Bank and Golan Heights, and in the Sinai Peninsula and Gaza Strip until Israel's withdrawal from those two areas in 1982 and 2005 respectively. The explicit goal of the settlers is to reclaim their God-given real estate from the Palestinians, often referred to as "Ishmaelites."[11] According to this view, the Palestinians who lived and who continue to live there have no right to the land: they are descendants of Ishmael, Abraham's firstborn son who had been rejected in favor of his half-brother Isaac.[12]

But who were the original Ishmaelites? In Genesis, several of the names of Ishmael's sons are the names of places in northern Arabia known from nonbiblical sources, so we should locate these more distant relatives of the Israelites in that region.[13] But this does not necessarily correspond to present-day usage: the Arabs of biblical times are not necessarily the same as modern Arabs. Here we enter upon issues of ethnic and national identity. The shorthand summary that all modern Arabs are originally from the Arabian peninsula has no historical basis. Pan-Arab nationalism, to be sure, simplistically asserts that all Arabs are one nation. Perhaps it is best simply to define an Arab as someone who speaks Arabic, the language that Muslims brought to the territories they took over in the Middle East and North Africa, just as the Greeks had done centuries before. Recently scientists compared the genomes of ninety-nine modern inhabitants of Lebanon with those of five ancient Canaanite skeletons from Sidon on the southern Lebanese coast dating to about 2700 BCE. They concluded that "present-day Lebanese derive most of their ancestry from a Canaanite-related population, which therefore implies substantial genetic continuity in the Levant at least since the Bronze Age."[14] Presumably the same would be true of Palestinian Arabs, that is, that they, too, are descended from the original Canaanites. This would mean that their claim to the land is as old as that of the Jews, presuming that ancient lineage is at all relevant for modern title to land.

A biblical text frequently used by ultrareligious Zionists is one from the book of Isaiah discussed earlier (see page 69). This passage speaks of Jerusalem becoming the goal of pilgrimage of all nations, because from it "teaching [torah] will go out, and Yahweh's word from Jerusalem" (Isaiah 2:3). But biblical prophetic texts were written for particular ancient audiences in particular historical circumstances. Although sometimes using extravagant and even fantastic language, they were not encoded revelations of a far-distant future, to be intelligible only then. The biblical writers were not writing for us, but for their own contemporaries. This is admittedly a very low, minimalist view of the inspired character of scripture: God is not its author, and it is not a detailed account of what would happen in the eleventh or seventeenth or twenty-first century. But that is not the view of modern Jewish and Christian fundamentalists. They find in the Bible a detailed blueprint for the present as well as the future: all was foreseen by God and predicted in his scriptures.

Thus, for ultrareligious Zionists, the return of Jews of the Diaspora to the Promised Land and the Israeli capture of the West Bank and East Jerusalem in 1967 was the onset of the redemption of Israel, God's chosen people. Through Israel, the world will be redeemed and this will culminate in the coming of the Messiah, all in fulfillment of biblical prophecy. So, the younger Rabbi Kook preached that the liberation of the "land of the Patriarchs," where much of the biblical epic had played out, was "a determination of divine politics that no mortal politics can overcome."[15] Eleazar Waldman, a student of the younger Rabbi Kook and a founder of Gush Emunim, put it this way in 1983:

> The Redemption is not only the Redemption of Israel but the Redemption of the whole world. But the Redemption of the world *depends* on the Redemption of Israel. From this derives our moral, spiritual, and cultural influence over the entire world. The blessing will come to all of humanity from the people of Israel living in the whole of its land.[16]

Israelis who have disagreed with the views of ultrareligious Zionists have been labeled heretics and traitors, with some even calling for their deaths. In 1995, a few weeks after Yitzhak Rabin, Israel's prime minister, and Yasser Arafat, chairman of the Palestine Liberation Organization, signed the second of the Oslo Accords, which in theory at least allowed for Palestinian sovereignty over most of the West Bank and Gaza, Rabin was assassinated. His assassin, Yigal Amir, had close connections with the settler movement. Non-Israelis, both Jews and non-Jews, who have opposed the virtually consistent policy of Israeli governments about the settlements since 1967, have also been denounced as self-hating Jews and anti-Semites, respectively.[17]

But for ultrareligious Zionists, recognition of Palestinian territorial sovereignty is not negotiable, because Jewish control of the original land of Canaan is divinely ordained. Harold Fisch, himself a religious Zionist and former rector of Bar-Ilan University, put it this way:

> From scattered colonies to a National Home; from a National Home to a state in a fraction of the land; and from that to the liberation of the land of Israel as a whole on behalf of the Jewish people: here was a process that we did not initiate; at each stage we had no option but to respond to a demand made on us; we are manifestly coerced by the logic of tragedy and redemption.[18]

The concept of a chosen people, originally one group's self-definition as superior to others, has again become God's immutable decree.

A similar reading of the Bible as God's detailed revelation about our own times is shared by fundamentalist Christians, many of whom are also ardent Zionists.[19] The belief that the return of Jews to the Promised Land was a sign that Christ's return would soon occur is not modern. We find it frequently among Reformation-era writers and among American thinkers, too. As previously mentioned, in his 1783 sermon "The United States Elevated to Glory and Honor," Ezra Stiles referred to "the reassembling of the Jews" as a prerequisite for the Second Coming of Christ. In the nineteenth century, several groups, drawing a conclusion from their reading of the biblical prophets that the Second Coming would soon occur, moved at various times to the "Holy Land" in order to be on the scene when Jesus returned to it. One such group, led by Anna and Horatio Spafford, moved from Chicago to Jerusalem in 1881 and established a utopian, philanthropic, and from time to time celibate society there. Eventually they moved to a large estate, in the neighborhood of East Jerusalem still known as the American Colony.[20] But this early Christian Zionism was theoretical, not political.

The growth of the Christian Zionist movement in the late nineteenth and early twentieth centuries was linked with an increase in apocalyptic eschatology among some Protestants, who saw the return of Jews to the Promised Land as a sure sign that the end-time was approaching. For them, it is the fulfillment of passages such as this, addressed to "the house of Israel" by the prophet Ezekiel in Yahweh's name: "I will take you from all the nations and I will gather you from all the lands and I will bring you to your own soil" (Ezekiel 36:24).[21]

The establishment of Israel in 1948 and especially the Israeli victories in the 1967 and 1973 wars provided further evidence that the Second Coming of Christ was imminent.[22] The largest Christian Zionist organization in the United States today is Christians United for Israel, founded in 1992, and since 2006 led by John Hagee, the pastor of an evangelical megachurch in San Antonio, Texas. On the basis of his interpretation of biblical prophecies, Hagee has proclaimed that "God is getting ready to change the course of human history once again."[23]

By the late twentieth century, ultrareligious Jewish Zionists and fundamentalist Christian Zionists shared both presuppositions and conclusions: for both groups, the return of Jews to Israel is only the first act in a drama that will culminate in the coming of the Messiah to Jerusalem. Both groups take the Bible literally—after all, it is God's word, and as such contains his plans for the rest of time. The biblical texts most often used for discerning the details of the divine plan are later prophetic and apocalyptic writings, especially Zechariah 9–14 and Daniel 7–12, as well as, for Christian Zionists, the book of Revelation in the New Testament. Often written in times of historical crisis, many of these writings are a sort of consolation literature for their original audiences, using the fantastic to describe a better future for those designating themselves as chosen. A scattered people will be returned to the Promised Land; a destroyed Jerusalem will be rebuilt, with its restored temple more resplendent than ever; a king in David's line will rule again, inaugurating an era of peace and prosperity. Late in the biblical period, such dreams of good times ahead were combined with a growing belief in immortality after death, at least for the chosen, "the people of the holy ones of the Most High" (Daniel 7:27).[24] Although this new era would be preceded by a period of trial and tribulation, it would end wonderfully, as the second-century BCE book of Daniel predicts:

> There will be a time of distress, such as never has been since a nation existed until that time. And at that time your people will be rescued, everyone found written in the book. Many of those who sleep in the dust of the earth will awaken, some to eternal life, and some to shame, to eternal abhorrence. Those who are wise will shine like the firmament's shining, and those who cause many to be righteous will be like the stars forever and ever. (Daniel 12:1–3)

Whether in this life or the next, the future will resolve God's apparent lack of care for and failure to keep his promises to his chosen people in the past and in the present by postponing that future to another realm or another mode of existence.

Among Christian Zionists there is a spectrum of beliefs about the details of the end-time. We find dispensationalists, premillenarians, millenarians, amillenarians, postmillenarians, and so on, in as bewildering and fluid a variety as Israeli political parties. Many of the differences concern timing. When will all this happen? Some apocalyptic literature is precise, or at least appears to be: "All these things will be accomplished . . . in a time, times, and a half" (Daniel 12:7), whatever that means. Elsewhere in Daniel we have somewhat clearer figures: 2,300 evenings and mornings (that is, probably, 1,150 days; 8:14), 1,290 days (12:11), and 1,335 days (12:12). If we take these literally, despite their inconsistencies, then for the author of the book of Daniel this was apparently to be very soon, in his own lifetime.[25] The same is true of apocalyptic passages in the Gospels. According to them, Jesus reportedly said: "Amen I say to you, this generation will not pass away before all these things are accomplished" (Mark 13:30; compare Matthew 24:34; Luke 21:32).

The timetable in the book of Revelation is even more complicated. It interprets the "time, times, and a half" of Daniel as forty-two months (that is, three and a half years; Revelation 11:2; 13:5) of tribulation, to be followed by a thousand-year reign of Christ (Revelation 20:4–6), then a great battle in which the forces of evil are defeated (Revelation 20:7–10), and finally "a new heaven and a new earth" and "the new Jerusalem" (Revelation 21:1–2), all of which the author, like other early Christians, expected would be soon.[26] No matter that Jesus himself reportedly warned that even he did not know when the end-time would be (Mark 13:32): believers through the ages, especially those on the fringe, have identified the prophecies as fulfilled in their own times, and fundamentalist Christians today are doing the same. For them, we clearly are on the very cusp of the end of the world.

Given their similar views both about the biblical writings as divine pronouncements and about the nature of the times in which we live, it is hardly surprising that for several decades ultrareligious Jewish Zionists, especially in Israel, and fundamentalist Christian Zionists, especially in the United States, have been political allies. But it is an unholy alliance. For Christian fundamentalists the Messiah is not the Jewish Messiah—rather, he is Jesus, who will soon return to the earth to complete the divine plan by establishing his kingdom that will have no end, as both Luke 1:33 and the Nicene Creed of the fourth century CE put it. That plan is thought to be laid out in detail not just in the Jewish scriptures, but also in the New Testament. Either before or at Jesus's return, Jews must convert to Christianity; those who do not will be ruthlessly slaughtered by divine decree. Here is one of the biblical proof texts: "In all the land—oracle of

Yahweh—two-thirds in it will be cut off and will perish, and one-third will be left in it" (Zechariah 13:8). How many will be left? According to some Christian Zionists' interpretations of Revelation 7:4–8, this will be a remnant of only 144,000; if all other Jews are to die, then the result will be a second Holocaust. For right-wing Israelis to align themselves with Christian Zionists for political advantage is at least naïve, if not cynical.

Both Jewish and Christian fundamentalists indulge in a facile interpretation of the Bible as written not for its original audiences, but as a kind of secret code that only they have truly deciphered. According to their readings, although mutually inconsistent in detail, the land God promised to Abraham belongs only to the Jews, and they have now reclaimed it as God had planned. The Palestinian Arabs are not chosen, and have no share in the Promised Land, as God decreed long ago: they are Ishmaelites.

But the mutual antagonism of Jews and Arabs, of Israelis and Palestinians, is not the only biblical model. Although one source in Genesis describes Ishmael as "a wild ass of a man, his hand against everyone and everyone's hand against him," who "will live in opposition to all his brothers" (Genesis 16:12),[27] another source has God bless Ishmael, promising that he too will be a "great nation" (Genesis 21:13, 18). Especially apropos is the account of Abraham's funeral: "His sons Isaac and Ishmael buried him in the cave of Machpelah" (Genesis 25:9). Perhaps Israelis and Arabs, who both identify Abraham as their common ancestor, should reenact this moment, when the two brothers came together in peace to honor their father. And perhaps Christians, who also claim Abraham as their spiritual ancestor, should stop taking sides with either group.

10

IMMIGRANTS AND REFUGEES, IDEALS AND REALITIES

WE TURN NOW TO ANOTHER INTERSECTION of biblical and contemporary thought, how those who proclaim themselves to have been divinely chosen treat immigrants and refugees. In the book of Genesis, Abraham identified himself to the Hittites at Hebron, in the Promised Land of Canaan, as an immigrant (in Hebrew, *ger*).[1] According to the narrative, Abraham's extended family had no intention of returning to their homeland in Mesopotamia, so he was an immigrant in the modern sense, one who had moved permanently. Later, because of a famine in Canaan, Abraham left it for Egypt, where he was also a *ger*, but here "temporary resident" (usually translated "resident alien") is a better translation for that word, because Abraham may have intended to—and in fact did eventually—return to Canaan.[2]

Abraham's journeys between Canaan and Egypt anticipate those of Jacob and his extended family from Canaan to Egypt, also because of a famine, and that of their descendants, the Israelites, back to Canaan in the Exodus from Egypt. According to the book of Deuteronomy, at the late spring harvest festival of Weeks (Shavuot or Pentecost), the Israelites are to proclaim:

> A wandering Aramean was my father. He went down to Egypt and was a temporary resident there, few in number, but there he became a great and very populous nation. When the Egyptians

treated us harshly and oppressed us, . . . Yahweh brought us out
of Egypt . . . and he brought us into this place and he gave us this
land. (Deuteronomy 26:5–9)

In its early history, this group was an itinerant family: sometimes they
were immigrants, sometimes they were what we would call refugees,
and sometimes they were temporary residents.[3] But once the Israelites
arrived in the Promised Land from Egypt, they assumed the status of
"native-born," and the Canaanites became "resident aliens" in their
former territory.

Biblical law recognizes four principal social classes: the native-born;
immigrants or temporary residents; foreigners; and slaves. The
native-born were the Israelites themselves, who had a special obligation to each other. [4] To use biblical terminology, a fellow Israelite was
one's neighbor, to whom one had special obligations—"You should
love your neighbor as yourself" (Leviticus 19:18)—surpassed only by
those of direct kinship.[5]

Immigrants and temporary residents were persons living outside
their native territory, either permanently or temporarily, respectively.[6] Immigrants in ancient Israel were subject to most civil and
religious laws: the idea of "an eye for an eye" applied to them, as did
Sabbath observance, purity laws, and the prohibition against blasphemy.[7] They were permitted to celebrate the Passover, provided that
they had been circumcised, as well as other festivals.[8] They were not
permitted to own land, and thus were often agricultural laborers.[9]
They could be made slaves.[10]

Foreigners were persons who had left their own territory for a
while, but usually intended to return there.[11] Mercenaries were often
foreigners, as were some merchants.[12] If foreigners borrowed money
from Israelites, they could be charged interest, whereas Israelites were
not supposed to charge each other interest.[13] Unlike immigrants,
some foreign mercenaries could apparently own land.[14] Like immigrants, however, foreigners could also be made slaves.[15]

Slavery was an established institution in ancient Israel, as it
was throughout the ancient world. Like immigrants and foreigners,

prisoners of war could also become slaves, and children of slaves generally were also enslaved.[16] Slaves were their owner's property, like real estate, livestock, and gold and silver.[17] Male slaves of Israelites were circumcised, which enabled them to celebrate Passover.[18] According to Deuteronomy's version of the Sabbath commandment, the Sabbath was instituted so that slaves could rest.[19] In the Exodus, Yahweh freed the Israelites from Egyptian slavery, and in effect they became Yahweh's slaves, so they should not enslave each other.[20] Still, fellow Israelites could be subjected to debt slavery, in theory only for a limited term unless they consented to be slaves in perpetuity.[21]

The categories of exiles and refugees are closely related to that of immigrants. In biblical times as ever since, people have been deported or fled from their place of origin, because of war, famine, or persecution. We find exiles and refugees repeatedly in the Bible, beginning with Adam and Eve, who were banished from Eden never to return. Abraham, Isaac, and Jacob and their families were sometimes refugees, either because of famine or because, as in Jacob's case when he fled from Esau, they feared for their lives. Similarly, Moses was a refugee when he fled from Egypt to Midian; David was a refugee when he was on the run from Saul; Mary, Jesus, and Joseph were refugees when they went down to Egypt to prevent Herod from killing Jesus; and other characters in biblical narrative can also be called refugees. From the late eighth to the early sixth centuries BCE, invading Assyrian and Babylonian armies forcibly deported large numbers of Israelites from their homelands; nearly all of the occurrences of the word for "exile" in the Hebrew Bible refer to these imperial population transfers.[22] One of the reliefs from the Assyrian king Sennacherib's palace at Nineveh depicts Judean refugees from the city of Lachish being exiled in 701 BCE.

Some refugees leave their own territory for another voluntarily, although reluctantly. There is no ancient Hebrew word that corresponds exactly to the modern legal category of refugee; the closest means "escapee" or "survivor."[23] Like the families of Abraham, Isaac, and Jacob, who left Canaan because of famines, so, too, in the book of Ruth did Naomi, Elimelech, and their two sons leave Bethlehem in Judah for the territory of Moab to the east because of a famine. All were what we would call refugees.

Runaway slaves are also refugees of a sort. According to biblical law, fugitive slaves should not be returned to their owners.[24] This contrasts with some other ancient Near Eastern laws, in which fugitive slaves are like straying animals, whose finders were required to return them to their owners.

Finally, according to biblical law, several cities belonging to the priesthood were set apart as places of asylum for anyone guilty of involuntary manslaughter, so that the next of kin of the person killed could not take blood vengeance.[25] The designated cities are often called "cities of refuge," so we may identify those seeking asylum in them as refugees.

The preceding paragraphs summarize biblical laws written down over many centuries, and it is difficult to determine exactly when and how they were applied. But one consistent feature in all layers of tradition is that immigrants were among the most vulnerable in Israelite society, repeatedly grouped with widows and orphans as those most in need of protection.[26] As motivation for doing so, again laws from all layers of tradition appeal to the Israelites' experience in Egypt, urging them to imitate Yahweh, "who loves immigrants, giving them food and clothing, so you should love immigrants, for you were immigrants in the land of Egypt" (Deuteronomy 10:18–19). Not only are they to love their neighbors—that is, their fellow Israelites—as themselves, but they should also "love immigrants as yourself, for you were immigrants in the land of Egypt" (Leviticus 19:34) and therefore "you know the heart of an immigrant" (Exodus 23:9). This special status for immigrants is virtually absent in other ancient Near Eastern legal collections.[27]

The New Testament continues the Israelite emphasis on care for the most vulnerable and the most needy. Matthew's gospel has Jesus describes the final judgment, when Jesus himself, "the son of man," returns in glory as a king. He will separate all peoples into two groups, as a shepherd separates sheep and goats. The sheep, at his right, are told they will inherit the kingdom that has been prepared for them from the creation of the world. Why? The king answers: "I was hungry and you gave me something to eat; I was thirsty and you gave me something to drink; I was a stranger and you welcomed me; I was naked and you gave me clothing; I was sick and you cared for me; I was in prison and you visited me."[28] They will ask him when did they ever see him hungry, or thirsty, or as a stranger, or naked, or sick, or in prison. And he will reply, "Whenever you did it to one of the least of my brothers, you did it to me." The goats, at his left, are told they will suffer eternal damnation, because they did not help and care for those in need (Matthew 25:31–46).

The moral obligation to care for those in need is also the message of Jesus's parable of "the good Samaritan," found in the gospel of Luke.[29] In the narrative context of the parable, a lawyer—an expert in the law of Moses, the Torah—asks Jesus what he should do to inherit eternal life. Jesus, as often, answers with a question: "What is written in the law? How do you read it?" The lawyer replies, "You should love the Lord your god with all your heart and with all your soul and with all your strength and with all your mind, and your neighbor as yourself" (Luke 10:27), combining words from Deuteronomy 6:5 (the Shema), and Leviticus 19:18.[30] Jesus agrees. But then, in a kind of Socratic dialogue, the lawyer asks another question: "Who is my neighbor?"

Jesus replies with this story. An unidentified man was traveling on the road from Jerusalem, some 2,500 feet above sea level, to Jericho, over 800 feet below sea level. The road, about eighteen miles long, went through rugged and desolate terrain where bandits often lurked. Some such bandits mugged and robbed the man, leaving him seriously injured and alone. Three passersby encountered him. The first two, a priest and a Levite, kept going, for reasons not given.[31] But the third, a Samaritan, gave him first aid, using wine as an antiseptic and oil as a salve. Then he put him on his own animal and took him to an inn where he tended to him. The next day he gave the innkeeper money to care for the injured man, promising to pay more when he returned. Jesus ends the story with a question that echoes the lawyer's: "Which of these three was a neighbor to the man who fell among bandits?" (Luke 10:36).

In the first century CE, as in preceding centuries, Jews and Samaritans were often at odds, even hostile to each other, as the New Testament and other sources indicate.[32] In making the hero of the parable a hated Samaritan, Jesus is being deliberately provocative, undercutting prejudice and stereotyping. Jesus's reversal of the lawyer's question provides an important insight into the concept of love of neighbor. Loving one's neighbor as oneself, Jesus implies, means putting the neighbor in the center: the question should not be who is my neighbor, but to whom am I obligated to be a neighbor. The answer is anyone in need, even an enemy: One saying of Jesus that scholars think is his own words is "Love your enemies" (Matthew 5:44; Luke 6:27).[33]

Love of one's enemies was not an innovation of Jesus. It is implied, for example, in the Torah:

> When you happen upon your enemy's ox or his donkey straying, you should return it to him. When you see the donkey of someone who hates you collapsed under its load, and you might want to refrain from helping him, you should help him with it. (Exodus 23:4–5)[34]

The book of Proverbs has a similar view:

> If someone who hates you is hungry, give him food to eat,
>   and if he is thirsty, give him water to drink
>   (25:21).[35]

But neither in the Hebrew Bible nor in the New Testament is an explicit motive given for loving one's enemies. Is it pure altruism or enlightened self-interest—those who help their enemies end up making friends of them—or both? In any case, as in the parable of the Samaritan, even an enemy can be a neighbor who should be loved. Jesus seems to have made this ancient idea central to his teaching.[36]

■   ■   ■

Groups identifying themselves as divinely chosen have often been immigrants and refugees, fleeing famine, persecution, or enslavement. Sometimes, too, they have been forced into exile. It is profoundly ironic that such groups, who have known from their own experience what it is like to be slaves, immigrants, and refugees, whose self-proclaimed ideal is special care for those in similar situations, have often treated others not as they themselves would like to have been treated but rather as they had been treated, making others slaves, immigrants, and refugees. Although Abraham himself had been a refugee, at Sarah's insistence he made refugees of his secondary wife Hagar and their son Ishmael; he sent her away, just as Ezra and Nehemiah, themselves returnees from exile, did to the "foreign" wives and children of Judean men.

According to the book of Joshua, when the inhabitants of Gibeon, a small town about six miles northwest of Jerusalem, learned how Joshua and the Israelites had defeated the cities of Jericho and Ai and slaughtered all their inhabitants, the Gibeonites concocted a scheme in order to escape a similar fate. They were implausibly familiar with a law in the book of Deuteronomy, which commands the Israelites to spare their more distant neighbors if they are willing to surrender, subjecting them only to forced labor.[37] The Gibeonites put on worn-out clothes and sandals. With worn-out sacks for their donkeys, patched wineskins, and dry and crumbly bread, they arrived at the Israelite camp, claiming to have come from far away. The Israelites made an irrevocable peace treaty with them, so when the ruse was discovered, they had to keep it, and could not subject them to the extermination ban. But they were made slaves—"woodcutters and water haulers"—for the community and its sanctuary in perpetuity (Joshua 9:27). Moreover, according to the book of Judges, the Israelites, themselves only recently rescued from Egyptian servitude, subjected other groups of Canaanites to forced labor as well.[38] Their own experience of slavery and oppression did not, at least according to the narrative, inspire the Israelites to treat others as Yahweh had treated them.

Slavery is enshrined even in the Ten Commandments. Although they begin, "I am Yahweh your god, who brought you out from the land of Egypt, from the house of slaves" (Exodus 20:2; Deuteronomy 5:1), they go on to prohibit "coveting" any of one's neighbor's property, including his slaves (and his wife). Abraham, Jacob, Solomon, and Job were all slaveowners, and the exiles who returned from Babylonia reportedly had thousands of slaves.[39]

Slavery is also unchallenged in the New Testament. Nowhere is Jesus reported as suggesting that slavery is abhorrent. In his letter to Philemon, Paul does not tell his correspondent to set his runaway slave free. In fact, 1 Peter instructs slaves to obey their masters even if they are harsh.[40] Only in the latest of the scriptures of the Abrahamic religions do we see the beginning of a change of view: the Qur'an describes the "steep path" as one that involves freeing of slaves (90:12–13), and says that one of the purposes of giving alms, the third pillar of the faith, is to free slaves (9:60). Still, slavery was a Muslim practice for many centuries to come, as it was among Jews and Christians. Because of the Bible's views on slavery, during the debates about abolition in the United States in the nineteenth century the pro-slavery side could appeal to the Bible in support of its position, while the abolitionists could only use vague texts, like the "Golden Rule": "Do unto others as you would have them do unto you."[41]

In postbiblical times, Jews have also repeatedly been exiles and refugees. Here is just a sample of many instances. The Roman emperor Hadrian expelled Jews from Jerusalem after the Second Jewish Revolt in 135 CE. In 1492, Jews, along with Muslims, were expelled from Spain if they refused to convert to Christianity. Jews were banned from England from 1290 until Oliver Cromwell allowed them to return in 1656, at least in part because of apocalyptic expectations.[42] Cromwell and other Puritans, like some in New England, believed that the Second Coming was about to occur. For them, the execution of King Charles I in 1649 and the establishment of the Puritan Commonwealth of England, Ireland, and Scotland signaled the beginning of the end-time, which would happen in 1656. This date was based on a saying attributed to Jesus: "But as the days of Noe were, so shall also the coming of the Son of Man be" (Matthew 24:37; King

James Version); in one reckoning of biblical chronology, the Flood in Genesis 6–9 occurred 1,656 years after the creation of the world, so the Second Coming could logically be expected in the year 1656 CE. That event needed to be preceded by the conversion of the Jews, who were therefore allowed to return to England so that they could be made Christians. Pogroms in Russia inspired Herzl to found the Zionist movement to give the Jewish people a homeland where they would not be persecuted and could control their own destiny. The Nazi "final solution" that resulted in the flight of hundreds of thousands of Jews from Europe and the murder of some six million was the most horrible of the repeated attacks on Jews throughout history. This Holocaust soon became the catalyst for the establishment of the modern state of Israel in 1948.

In a double tragedy, the subsequent wars between neighboring Arab states and Israel, itself increasingly a country of refugees, led to the creation of other refugee problems. One was the influx into Israel of nearly a million Jews from predominantly Muslim Middle Eastern countries. Jewish communities had not just survived but often flourished for many centuries in Syria, Iraq, Iran, Yemen, Egypt, and North Africa. But Zionist activity in those countries along with opposition in them to the establishment of Israel, often accompanied by violent treatment of Jews, resulted in the majority of the Jews there immigrating to Israel in the years following 1948; many others immigrated to Europe and to North and South America. In Iraq, where Jews had lived since the Assyrian and Babylonian deportations of the Israelites in the eighth and sixth centuries BCE, some 123,000 Jews, more than 90 percent of the Jewish population, immigrated to Israel between 1949 and 1951.[43] In Yemen, some 44,000 Yemenite Jews were airlifted to Israel in 1949 and 1950.[44] Today, fewer than a hundred Jews are estimated to be living in Iraq and Yemen combined. This pattern repeated itself in other Arab countries, as well as in Iran and, to some extent, Turkey.

Another refugee problem resulting from Israel's independence was that of Palestinian Arabs in territory that Israel now claimed as its own. Until 1948, Lydda (earlier biblical Lod, modern Arabic al-Ludd), about ten miles southeast of Tel Aviv, was a Palestinian town with a population of about 20,000. That changed dramatically in July 1948, when several hundred inhabitants were killed by Israeli defense forces over three days, and nearly all of the rest were forced to flee to the Jordanian line and were eventually relocated in a refugee camp north of Jerusalem in the West Bank of what was then part of Jordan.[45] The town was then resettled by Jewish refugees, mostly from Muslim countries which they had been forced to leave; it is now the location of Israel's major airport. Lydda is just one of the more notorious examples of how Zionist refugees from persecution and prejudice in Europe and survivors of the Nazi Holocaust created a new group of refugees, the Palestinian Arabs. In the 1948 war between the newly founded state of Israel and its Arab neighbors, some 700,000 Palestinians were displaced, and in the 1967 war, several hundred thousand more. These refugees and their descendants, now numbering about 5.3 million, live in some fifty-nine camps in Jordan, Lebanon, Syria, the West Bank, and the Gaza Strip under the care of the United Nations Relief and Works Agency for Palestine Refugees in the Near East (UNRWA); this does not include the nearly 2 million now living in Europe, North and South America, and Australia.

The Puritans of Massachusetts were no less inconsistent. Although themselves exiles and dissenters, they would brook no dissent, and in 1635 formally exiled Roger Williams to Rhode Island for his dissident views, including about when to give thanks at mealtimes.[46] Moreover, although themselves refugees, they and subsequent generations of Americans of European origin systematically dispossessed, relocated, and killed Native Americans, rationalizing their treatment of them by appealing to the Bible: if they were God's new Israel, then they could treat the indigenous inhabitants of the land just as the Israelites of old treated the Canaanites.

Archaeology and anthropology had not yet been invented, and, after all, the Bible was, most Jewish and Christian thinkers believed, divinely revealed and thus a true and complete history of the human species. As such, it must explain who these Native Americans were. So, all that was necessary to find out the origin of the Indians was to comb the pages of scripture and to identify the Indians with one of the many groups that God himself had reportedly dispersed.

Some identified the Indians as descendants of the people whose languages the Lord had confused and whom he had scattered after the destruction of the tower of Babel.[47] This explained why the Indians spoke so many languages, unrelated both to each other and to European languages. Some thought they were the descendants of Noah's accursed son Ham, along with indigenous Africans.[48] Still others, like Ezra Stiles, thought that they were Canaanites who had fled the Promised Land during the Israelite conquest, some having been "wafted across the Atlantic," while others headed east and crossed the Bering Strait.[49] In all these cases, the Indians were clearly divinely rejected, deserving of whatever the chosen chose to do to them.

Some Puritans, however, thought that the Indians were descended from the "ten lost tribes of Israel" who had been deported from the northern kingdom of Israel by the Assyrians in the late eighth century BCE.[50] According to some interpretations of biblical texts, a prerequisite for Christ's return was the conversion of the Jews, before the Gentiles, and their return to the Promised Land.[51] If the Native Americans were descendants of the lost tribes, then converting them would hasten the Second Coming of Christ.

Among those who subscribed to the lost tribes theory was John Eliot, who had immigrated from England to Massachusetts in 1631 and who saw in the Indians "the posterity of the dispersed and rejected Israelites."[52] This "apostle to the Indians" translated the Bible into the local dialect of Algonquian and established towns of "praying Indians." But despite their having become Christians, several hundred of these Native Americans were interned in 1675 during King Philip's War on islands in Boston harbor, where two-thirds of them died from hunger and disease. Eliot was a notable exception in his efforts to treat Indians fairly and to learn their languages, as also was Roger Williams, who wrote:

> Boast not proud English, of thy birth and blood,
> Thy brother Indian is by birth as good.

Of one blood God made him, and thee and all,
As wise, as fair, as strong, as personal.[53]

The restoration of the British monarchy in 1660 dampened hopes that the Second Coming was imminent, although some continued to believe that the Native Americans were descendants of the dispersed Israelites. The Book of Mormon (1830) repeatedly makes the same claim.[54] In 1832, Harriet Livermore, a preacher and missionary to the Indians, wrote that at the Second Coming, which she initially thought would occur in 1847, when all Jews returned to the Holy Land:

How happy is Judah to meet his lost brethren,
Tribes of the red men from forests afar.[55]

By the nineteenth century, "scientific" evidence was produced that the Native Americans, like the Africans, were an inferior subspecies. This rationalized forcing them to move west so that their lands could be expropriated for an expanding United States. One horrifying example is the Indian Removal Act of 1830, which forced some 18,000 members of the Cherokee nation to walk from their homeland in the southeastern United States to the Indian Territory in what is now Oklahoma. Their perilous journey was along the "trail of tears," used by other Indian tribes before and after. In a letter to President Van Buren, Ralph Waldo Emerson opposed the expulsion of the Cherokees as "fraud and robbery," also describing "the painful labors of these red men to redeem their own race from the doom of eternal inferiority, and to borrow and domesticate in the tribe the arts and customs of the Caucasian race."[56]

Racism has been called America's original sin, evident not only in its appalling treatment of Native Americans and of slaves of African origin, but also in its immigration policies.[57] A growing and expanding country needs immigrants, but we want to preserve our identity, such as it is or as we imagine it should be. That the only really suitable immigrants are those who are like us is evident in the Naturalization

Act of the First Congress in 1790, which restricted citizenship to free white persons. This eliminated not only slaves and indentured servants, but also Indians and even freed slaves, as well as Asians and Africans. Subsequent federal laws implicitly and often explicitly continued this trend. Chinese immigrant laborers, essential to the Gold Rush in the mid-nineteenth century and to the building of the western part of the Transcontinental Railroad slightly later, were no longer welcome after these activities dwindled or were completed. So, in 1882, Congress passed and President Arthur signed the Chinese Exclusion Act, which banned immigrant laborers from China for ten years. The act was repeatedly renewed and was made permanent in 1902. The Immigration Act of 1924 further restricted immigration of Asians, as well as of Arabs, Africans, and southern and eastern Europeans. For example, according to the quotas set by the act, 57,000 immigrants from Germany were to be admitted annually, but only 4,000 from Italy; in contrast, at the beginning of the century an average of over 200,000 Italians had immigrated to the United States each year.[58] Even more restrictive was the granting of only a hundred immigrant visas each year to persons from all African countries.

The Immigration and Nationality Act of 1965 abolished the national-origins quotas, replacing them with one quota for each hemisphere and giving preference to skilled immigrants. But only 170,000 persons could be given immigrant visas. Spouses, children, and parents of United States citizens were exempt from the quotas, as were some spouses and children of permanent residents and some siblings of United States citizens.

The implicit rationale for our immigration policy has always been that we do not want to radically and quickly change the demographic makeup of the United States and thus its supposed cultural unity. But this has not in fact worked: nonwhites will be a majority nationwide before midcentury, and already are in several southwestern states, as well as in many metropolitan areas, including Dallas, Houston, Los Angeles, Miami, New York, San Diego, and San Francisco.[59] Currently proposed changes to immigration policy would attempt to reverse this trend, halving the number of visas granted and eliminating those for family unification (pejoratively called "chain migration"). Breaking up families instead of uniting them, as proposed changes to US immigration laws would do, is sadly reminiscent of the forced separation of wives and children from their husbands and fathers in Jerusalem during Nehemiah's governorship in the fifth century BCE. Together with increased "enforcement and removal"—that is, deportation—of hundreds of thousands of illegal aliens annually in the last decade, we have returned to an immigration policy that has correctly been labeled "American apartheid."[60]

On an island at the entrance to New York Harbor stands the Statue of Liberty, given to the United States by France in 1876 in connection with the centennial of the Declaration of Independence. In her sonnet "The New Colossus," written in 1883 to help finance the statue's pedestal, Emma Lazarus named it "Mother of Exiles," who famously cries out "with silent lips":

> Give me your tired, your poor,
> Your huddled masses yearning to breathe free,
> The wretched refuse of your teeming shore.
> Send these, the homeless, tempest-tost to me,
> I lift my lamp beside the golden door!

The sonnet recognizes that those most likely to immigrate to the United States are those whose lives in their countries of origin are distressed: they suffer from poverty, hunger, prejudice, or persecution. Such circumstances are much more likely to be present among lower classes, especially in developing countries. In other words, the wealthy and elite are much less likely to become immigrants.

The lofty ideals of the sonnet are belied both by Lazarus's views elsewhere and by American immigration policies since the founding of the republic. Lazarus's Jewish ancestors had immigrated to the United States in the eighteenth century. Although she was proud of being Jewish, she was nonobservant.[61] She was active in New York and London literary circles, and was friends with Henry James,

Robert Browning, and Ralph Waldo Emerson, whom she once visited in Concord.

The year before Lazarus wrote "The New Colossus," she became engaged with the plight of Russian Jews fleeing attacks on them in Russia instigated by alleged Jewish participation in the assassination of Czar Alexander II. Witnessing their condition on Wards Island in the East River in New York City, she became convinced that persecuted Jewish refugees needed a homeland of their own in Palestine, anticipating Herzl's views a decade later.

Lazarus's opinion of those refugees was inconsistent with the tone of her poem. Although she praised the "deeds of kindness done towards the poor, the suffering, the widow, the orphan, the stranger, the runaway slave" commanded in the Torah, the "colonization in groups or en masse in the United States" of these Russian Jews, her "oppressed and ignorant brethren" with "their grotesque masquerade-garments" would in her view lead to their extermination, because they would have to assimilate, giving up strict Sabbath observance and other medieval superstitions.[62] So even Emma Lazarus, although sympathetic to the suffering of her Jewish coreligionists, thought that they should not be admitted as immigrants to the United States: so much for "huddled masses yearning to breathe free."

The office of the United Nations High Commissioner for Refugees (UNHCR) estimates there are 68.5 million displaced people in the world today, 25.4 million of whom are officially registered as refugees. More than half of these refugees are under the age of eighteen.[63] In 2017, 65,109 (less than a quarter of 1 percent) of these refugees were resettled worldwide.[64]

The United States Refugee Act of 1980 limits the number of refugees to be admitted annually to 50,000, although in an emergency the president may increase that number. During the Reagan administration, the number of refugee admissions averaged about 80,000 a year. During the George H. W. Bush administration, it was about 108,000. During the Clinton administration, it was down to 76,000. During the George W. Bush administration, it was short of 48,000.

During the Obama administration, it was about 70,000.[65] According to the International Rescue Committee, the number in 2018 could be as low as 15,000.[66] Moreover, the Trump administration has announced plans to deport many hundreds of thousands who had been admitted to the United States with temporary protection status, mostly from Latin America, the Middle East, and Africa, or who had been brought here illegally as infants and children.

"The New Colossus" echoes the biblical ideals of many of the original English settlers of the United States, offering this country as a haven for those most in need. But the response of the United States government to the contemporary refugee crisis, some of which we caused, has been token at best. The biblical ideals that inspired the Puritans have been virtually abandoned, and the self-proclaimed chosen people have rejected those they deem not chosen. With her silent lips, the "mother of exiles" now proclaims, "You are not welcome here."

11

BEYOND TRIBALISM

IN THIS BOOK, I have been engaged in a kind of thought experiment: I have tried to evaluate claims of individuals and groups that they have been divinely chosen without presuming that the claims are true. Sometimes this is easy. In 1934, Julius Leutheuser, a pastor and one of the leaders of the "German Christians" during the Nazi era, echoing a frequent biblical phrase, asserted that "God's kingdom [*Reich*] and the German Reich made a covenant: 'I will be your God and you will be my people.'"[1] At the time, few people outside Germany would have taken this as a statement of fact, and today even fewer anywhere would do so. Similarly, as I have suggested, no one any longer thinks that the Babylonian god Marduk chose Cyrus, the king of Persia, to rule Babylon as Cyrus claimed: that is a myth.

The same applies to American exceptionalism. In the context of claiming title to all of the Oregon Territory in the 1840s, up to the southern border of Russian Alaska at the latitude of 54°40', John L. O'Sullivan (of "manifest destiny" fame) asserted of all of North America that "the God of nature and of nations has marked it for our own."[2] But asserting it does not make it so, and despite O'Sullivan's mythical proclamation, in the end a political compromise was reached and the Forty-Ninth parallel, not the Fifty-Fourth, became the border between British North America and the United States.

Similarly, just because the Bible says so does not mean that Yahweh chose Cyrus to rule over Babylon and to allow Judeans exiled there to return to the Promised Land. Attributing victory and defeat or the rise and fall of empires to a deity is mythical, whether that deity is Marduk, Jupiter, or the biblical god. The claim that an individual or a group has been divinely chosen is also mythical. In other words, neither Abraham nor Jacob, neither ancient Israel nor the early Christian church, neither David, nor Charlemagne, nor Henry VIII, nor George Washington were actually chosen by God.[3]

In my view gods do not choose people, either groups or individuals. Rather, people choose a god and then assert that that god has chosen them or their ancestors. The assertion enables them to identify themselves as superior to their neighbors, or their ancestors as superior to their neighbors' ancestors. They project onto their god their own self-importance. The myth of divine choice then becomes part of the group's tradition, frequently preserved in written form. Once the ancient Israelite and early Christian writings became authoritative scripture, later Jewish and Christian individuals and groups used those writings to rationalize their own claim that God had specially chosen them. Appropriated uncritically, the Bible has thus been used to reinforce exclusivity and superiority, with new myths based on old myths.

Those who embrace the myth of divine choice of some over others divide up the world with divine sanction into binary categories— we/they, chosen/not chosen, believers/infidels, saved/damned,—with pernicious effects. In biblical times and ever since, the myth has been invoked to rationalize prejudice and exclusion, to justify confiscating land, breaking up families, murdering individuals and whole populations, and wars of all kinds—so-called holy wars, when they are anything but that.

Religion is often identified as the cause of the wars that punctuate human history; in the twentieth century alone, religion has been blamed for the "troubles" in Ireland, the antagonism between India and Pakistan, the Iran–Iraq war of the 1980s, the Balkan wars of the 1990s, and so on to the present. My view, however, is that what ignites and fuels these conflicts is not religion, but tribalism, in which religion is only one of many intertwined markers, including gender, ethnicity, language, class, power, and national identity, that individuals and communities use to distinguish themselves from others. Conflicts are given a religious veneer, when in fact they are not just about religion, and certainly not divinely ordained.

Finally, let me return to the Bible. Although the belief that "all scripture is inspired by God" (2 Timothy 3:16) is uncritical, as a biblical scholar I have found the Bible to be inspiring: within its multiple layers I have found many intellectually and personally rewarding ideas. I have also found it challenging, continually requiring me to reexamine my own presuppositions as I try to interpret it.

The many named and often unnamed biblical writers produced their works over many centuries. Not surprisingly, then, the biblical writers often disagree. Moreover, they were writing for audiences of their own times; they were not writing for us. One of the many wonderful things about the Bible is that its layers are in a kind of creative tension, both authorizing and forcing its readers to make their own judgments about which version of a narrative, which commandments, which understandings of God to accept and which to abandon. To put it somewhat differently, like scriptures of other religions, and like the US Constitution, the words of the Bible are historically conditioned.[4] But they also contain noble truths that have proven to be timeless, the cumulative wisdom of more than a thousand years. Our ongoing task is to distinguish between those noble truths and other words that should no longer be heeded because they are no longer valid or true. One touchstone for making such a distinction might be universality and inclusiveness.

We should abandon the myth of divine chosenness, just as all of us have rejected the Bible's teachings on slavery, and more and more of us are coming to reject its teachings on such issues as the status of women, capital punishment, and same-sex relationships and gender identity.[5] Fundamentally, we are all one tribe, one species, with no group, ancient or modern, specially chosen.

In her discussion of the parable of the Good Samaritan, Amy-Jill Levine suggests that we might contemporize its message by modernizing its characters. Suppose we make the man who was mugged an

Israeli Jew, the first of the two passersby who ignored the victim a Jewish medic from the Israeli army and the second a member of the Israel/Palestine Mission Network of the Presbyterian Church (USA), a group whose goal is to support Palestinian rights and which has frequently been attacked for being one-sided. Then let us make the Samaritan who stopped and helped the man who had been attacked a Palestinian Muslim who belongs to the often-extremist Palestinian group Hamas. Such a contemporary reading of what we might now call "the parable of the Good Hamas Member," Levine suggests, provides a societal as well as a personal model of love of neighbor and especially of love of enemies.[6]

In the Middle East and beyond, our neighbors—those most in need, those whom above all we should help—are to be found on the roads of Europe, in overloaded boats on the Mediterranean, in drought-afflicted regions in sub-Saharan Africa, at the border between Mexico and the United States, in detention centers for illegal immigrants in the United States, in refugee camps, and in far too many other places worldwide. Some of them may have been or may even now be our enemies, but no matter: they are also our neighbors, whom we should love as we love ourselves.

So, some aspects of the biblical god are worth imitating, because they express our highest ideals. One is that he loves all equally, as the Bible itself occasionally says. According to the prophet Isaiah, in the future Yahweh himself will proclaim, "Blessed be my people Egypt, and Assyria the work of my hands, and Israel my inheritance" (Isaiah 19:25): Yahweh's blessing—his love—has no favorites; it extends not just to the Israelites, but also to the Egyptians and the Assyrians, the Israelites' principal enemies in Isaiah's time. And just as Yahweh's love is universal, especially for the most vulnerable, so also should ours be, especially for the most vulnerable, whether they are part of our group or not, whether they are our neighbors or even our enemies.

ACKNOWLEDGMENTS

THE IDEA FOR THIS BOOK began as a course I taught at Harvard Divinity School in 2011. I am grateful to my students in the course and my wonderful teaching fellow Hilary Kapfer for their insights, and patience. My agent, Steven Hanselman of LevelFiveMedia, has been as always helpful and supportive. My editor at Beacon Press, Amy Caldwell, has been indispensable in making this a better book. I thank them both.

I am grateful for the generosity of family members, friends, and colleagues who read various chapters of this work while it was in progress, especially Daniel Coogan, Elizabeth Coogan, Matthew Coogan, Michael Drons, and Natasha Simon. My constant reader, my wife, Pamela Hill, has read and reread the book with her unmatched insight and continuing encouragement, and I thank her most of all.

Unless otherwise indicated, all translations are my own.

NOTES

CHAPTER 1: PRESUPPOSITIONS

1. Conor Cruise O'Brien, *God Land: Reflections on Religion and Nationalism* (Cambridge, MA: Harvard University Press, 1988), 19 and passim.

2. I will not deal extensively with parallel claims in other cultures, such as Egypt, Rome, China, Japan, and Korea, because they are outside my primary focus.

3. *The Jewish Annotated New Testament*, 2d ed. (New York: Oxford University Press, 2017).

4. "Scripturam de novo integro et libero animo examinare," *Tractatus Theologico-Politicus*, Preface (online in: Library of Latin Texts, Series B [Turnhout, Belgium: Brepols, 2017]), 9.

5. *Histoire Critique du Vieux Testament*, Paris: 1678.

6. H. H. Rowley, *The Biblical Doctrine of Election* (London: Lutterworth, 1950), 15. The quotations that follow are on pages 39 and 161.

7. Joel S. Kaminsky, *Yet I Loved Jacob: Reclaiming the Biblical Concept of Election* (Nashville, TN: Abingdon, 2007), 191.

CHAPTER 2: ABRAHAM AND SONS

1. Actually, Abraham is not called "chosen" in Genesis; the only use of the Hebrew verb *bahar* ("to choose") for the divine choice of Abraham in particular is from a relatively late biblical source (Nehemiah 9:7). Many English translations render a word in Genesis 18:19 as "I have chosen him," but it literally means "I have known him," using another verb.

2. Other names for these mounds are *tel* (Modern Hebrew), *tepe* (Farsi), and *hüyük* (Turkish).

3. In the Jewish Bible, the books of Genesis through Kings. In the Christian Bible, the books of Genesis through Nehemiah.

4. Genesis 11:26–32.

5. Syria Emergency, UNHCR, http://www.unhcr.org/en-us/syria-emergency.html, accessed August 23, 2018.

6. Genesis 12:1–3.

7. *Jubilees* 12:1–15.

8. For example, Qur'an 19:41–49; 21:51–71; 26:69–89; 37:83–99.

9. Genesis 12:7.

10. Genesis 16:1–3.

11. See Deuteronomy 21:15–17.

12. Genesis 16:4–15.

13. Genesis 17:19; 21:1–3.

14. Genesis 19:30–38.

15. Genesis 35:22; 49:4.

16. Genesis 25:1–4; 25:13–16; 35:22–26; 36:1–5, 9–30, 40–43; 46:8–27.

17. Genesis 25:5, 9.

18. Genesis 25:21.

19. Numbers 12:1.

20. Genesis 4:8; 2 Samuel 13:28–29; 1 Kings 2:24–25.

21. Genesis 38:27–30. As in the story of the birth of Esau and Jacob, this birth narrative anticipates the prominence of the younger of the twins, showing that both belong to a common stock of literary motifs.

22. The original meaning of Esau's name is unknown, and the birth narrative offers no etymology, correct or not.

23. Genesis 25:29–34.

24. In Hebrew, Rebekah is spelled *ribqah*, with a different letter, although some wordplay may also be present here. No clear explanation is explicitly given for Rebekah's preference for Jacob. One of the latest layers of Genesis implicitly connects it with Esau's marriage to "Hittite women" (Genesis 26:34–35), also called "Canaanite women" (28:6–9). This layer dates from the sixth or fifth century BCE, and may reflect Ezra and Nehemiah's insistence on endogamy; see further discussion on pages 69–71.

25. That episode provides yet another etymology for Jacob's name. In that meeting at the Wadi Jabbok (in Hebrew, *yabboq*), Jacob (*ya'aqob*) wrestled (*ye'abeq*) with God. The episode also provides an explanation of Jacob's new name, Israel. His divine adversary tells him, "You will no longer be named Jacob, but Israel (*yisra'el*), for you have struggled (*sarita*) with gods (or "God"; *elohim*) and with men and you prevailed" (Genesis 32:28). The verb *sarah*, "to struggle," occurs only in these verses in Genesis and Hosea, and it is likely a folk etymology for the name "Israel." The last line of Hosea's summary of the wrestling match between Jacob and God is puzzling. Neither Jacob nor his divine adversary are described as weeping in Genesis 32, although Hosea may have drawn on an independent, alternate tradition. Another possibility is that the weeping refers to Jacob's encounter with Esau, when he returned from Aram; when they met, they both wept, and Jacob sought his brother's favor (Genesis 33:4, 8, 10).

26. Jacob's twelve sons (called "the sons of Israel" and named in Exodus 1:1–5) are the ancestors of the Israelite tribes. The Hebrew continues to use

the phrase "the sons of Israel," for their offspring; translators often render it "the children of Israel," "the people of Israel," or simply "the Israelites." (Following standard modern practice, I use the term "Israelites" for the ancient people and "Israelis" for the citizens of the modern state of Israel.)

27. For example, Numbers 20:14; Amos 1:11; Obadiah 10; Malachi 1:2.

28. See, for example, Jeremiah 25:9; 43:10.

29. Exodus 33:19.

30. Kaminsky, *Yet I Loved Jacob.*

31. Joseph A. Fitzmyer, *Romans: A New Translation with Introduction and Commentary* (New York: Doubleday, 1993), 563.

CHAPTER 3: HIS NAME IS JEALOUS

1. The relationship between Aaron and Moses—and among Aaron, Moses, and their sister Miriam—is inconsistently described. In later genealogies (Exodus 6:20; Numbers 26:59; 1 Chronicles 6:3; compare Micah 6:4) they are all children of the same parents, but in some cases, apparently only Aaron and Miriam are siblings (Exodus 15:20; compare Numbers 12:1).

2. The Hebrew usually translated "Red Sea" is literally *Reed* Sea, and likely means a swampy region in the eastern Nile Delta.

3. Genesis 12:15–20; 39–50; Exodus 1:8–23; 5–15.

4. Exodus 12:37–38. But compare Exodus 1:15, where two midwives are apparently enough to supply gynecological and obstetrical care to the Hebrew women.

5. See, for example, Psalm 68:5; Exodus 23:9; Deuteronomy 5:14–15; 24:17. For the translation "immigrant" of Hebrew *ger* for the more usual "resident alien," see pages 115 and 152n1.

6. See Exodus 4:22–23.

7. Exodus 9:12; 10:1; 10:20, 27; 11:10; 14:8.

8. Exodus 7:13, 22; 8:19; 9:35.

9. Exodus 8:15, 32; 9:34.

10. See Exodus 7:5, 17; 8:10, 22; 9:14, 29.

11. The traditional identification of Mount Sinai with the impressive (some 7,500 feet high) Jebel Musa (Arabic for "Mount Moses") at the southern tip of the Sinai Peninsula is first found in Jewish and Christian sources from early in the Common Era. No archaeological evidence of earlier occupation has been found there. Complicating the issue is that in some biblical sources the mountain of revelation is called Horeb and in others Paran, rather than Sinai. See also Galatians 4:25.

12. In some sources Moses's father-in-law is named Jethro, in others Reuel. Two or three names of mountains, two fathers-in-law, and perhaps two wives: all further evidence of variant traditions incorporated into the Bible in its final form.

13. In the Bible, see Genesis 32:29; Judges 13:17–18.

14. In Egyptian transcription, *yhw3*, roughly "yahu," which is a form of the divine name (as in Benjamin Netanyahu).

15. See also Habakkuk 3:3.

16. Exodus 18:12.

17. For example, Abraham: Genesis 12:7; 15:2; 24:7; Isaac: 26:2, 22; Jacob: 28:13; 32:9.

18. See Joshua 24:14; Ezekiel 20:7–8.

19. "Yahweh," which probably means "the one who causes to be" (that is, "the one who brings into being/creates") may originally have been another epithet of the god El.

20. Exodus 19:5; Deuteronomy 7:6; 14:2; 26:18; Psalm 135:4; Malachi 3:17. In 1 Chronicles 29:3 and Ecclesiastes 2:8, *segullah* means personal property, something like a private hoard; this is how related words are used in other Semitic languages.

21. The traditional Hebrew text reads "sons of Israel" (in Hebrew, *bene yisrael*) for "gods" (*bene elohim*), an obvious correction of an originally polytheistic text. But the original reading is preserved in the Dead Sea Scrolls and in ancient translations. Other biblical passages also mention these "sons of God," lesser deities in the heavenly court: Genesis 6:2; Psalms 29:1; 82:1, 6; 89:6; Job 1:6; 2:1; 38:7. Translators usually use a circumlocution for the phrase, such as "heavenly beings," except in Genesis 6:1, which is transparently mythological.

22. "Kingdom of priests" could also be translated "royal priesthood," which is how the Septuagint, the ancient translation of the Hebrew Bible into Greek, renders the phrase.

23. For example, Isaiah 2:3; 61:6.

24. For passion, see for example Song of Solomon 8:6; for envy, Genesis 26:14; for zeal, 1 Kings 19:14; Psalm 69:10; for sexual jealousy, Numbers 5:14, 29–30; Proverbs 6:34.

25. Hosea 1–3; Ezekiel 16; 23.

26. Although the Midianites also guide the Israelites on their journey north (see Numbers 10:29–32), later they will become one of the Israelites' archetypal enemies; see for example Numbers 31:1–12; Judges 6–8; Isaiah 10:26.

27. See Exodus 18:13–27; contrast Deuteronomy 1:9–18, where it is Moses, not his father-in-law, who initiates the judicial system.

28. See Joshua 24:14–15.

29. Deuteronomy 7:2, 16.

30. Joshua 8:26; 10:1, 28–40; 11:10, 14.

31. Such catalogues occur frequently in ancient literature (for example, Joshua 13–21, Book 2 of the *Iliad*, and, to some extent, Ezekiel 27): audiences liked to hear about themselves.

32. Deuteronomy 13:6–11.

CHAPTER 4: DIVINELY CHOSEN KINGS AND KINGDOMS

1. See also Deuteronomy 17:14–15.

2. Translated by Frans van Koppen in M. W. Chavalas, ed. *The Ancient Near East: Historical Sources in Translation* (Oxford, UK: Blackwell, 2006), 104.

3. See, for example, Jean-Jacques Glassner, *Mesopotamian Chronicles* (Atlanta: Society of Biblical Literature, 2004), 119, 121, 129, 147; Stephanie Dalley, *Myths from Mesopotamia*, rev. ed. (Oxford, UK: Oxford University Press, 2000), 201n6.

4. "When the august god Anu, king of the Annunaki, and the god Enlil, lord of heaven and earth, who determines the destinies of the land, allotted supreme power over all peoples to Marduk, the firstborn son of the god Ea, exalted him among the Igigi deities, named the city of Babylon with its august name and made it supreme within the regions of the world, and established for him within it eternal kingship whose foundations are as fixed as heaven and earth, at that time the gods Anu and Enlil, for the enhancement of the well-being of the people, named me by name: Hammurapi, the pious prince, who venerates the gods, to make justice to prevail in the land, to abolish the wicked and the evil, to prevent the strong from oppressing the weak, to rise like the sun-god Shamash over all humankind, to illuminate the land. I am Hammurapi the shepherd, selected by the god Enlil." Translated by Martha T. Roth, *Law Collections from Mesopotamia and Asia Minor*, 2d ed., Writings from the Ancient World 6 (Atlanta: Scholars Press, 1997), 76–77. Hammurapi resumes this theme in the epilogue to the Code: "The great gods having chosen me, I am indeed the shepherd who brings peace" (Roth, 133).

5. Translated by Paul-Alain Beaulieu in *The Context of Scripture*, vol. 2, ed. W. W. Hallo (Leiden: Brill, 2003), 309.

6. Translated by Mordechai Cogan in Hallo, *The Context of Scripture*, 2:315.

7. *Vae, . . . puto deus fio* (Suetonius, *Lives of the Caesars*, 8, *The Deified Vespasian* [translated by J. C. Rolfe; Loeb Classical Library 38; Cambridge, MA: Harvard University Press, 1914] XXIII.4, page 304.).

8. An incomplete Canaanite epic from Ugarit in northwestern Syria features a king, Kirta, one of whose epithets is "son of El," the Canaanite high god. In one episode, Kirta becomes deathly ill, and his children wonder how this can be:

How can Kirta be called El's son,

> the offspring of the Kind and Holy One?
> Or do gods die?
>> Will the Kind One's offspring not live on?

(Translated by Michael D. Coogan and Mark S. Smith in *Stories from Ancient Canaan* [Louisville, KY: Westminster John Knox, 2nd ed., 2012], 87–88).

9. "Today" presumably means the day of the coronation ritual. Another biblical example of divine adoption at coronation is Isaiah 9:6, "Unto us a child is born . . . ," in which the council of the gods welcomes a new member into their midst. For other designations of the king as "son of God," see, for example, 2 Samuel 7:14, and Psalm 89:26–27 (discussed on pages 52–53).

10. The Wisdom of Solomon is a late first-century BCE or early first-century CE Jewish writing, which, although not in the Jewish canon, was part of all Christian Bibles until the Reformation, when Protestants relegated it and other relatively late books to the Apocrypha.

11. See also Proverbs 8:15–16; Daniel 2:21; 1 Peter 2:13–14.

12. "Carolus serenissimus Augustus, a Deo coronatus, magnus et pacificus imperator, Romanum gubernans imperium, qui et per misericordiam Dei rex Francorum et Langobardorum"; R. H. C. David, A History of Medieval Europe from Constantine to Saint Louis, 3rd ed. (New York: Longman, 2005), 166.

13. See http://media.gettyimages.com/photos/title-page-of-the-great-bible-1539-first-authorised-english-of-the-picture-id173275879.

14. Cromwell was beheaded the following year on charges of treason and heresy. Cranmer was burned at the stake for heresy in 1556, under the Catholic Queen Mary I.

15. Inveni virum iuxta cor meum qui facit omnes voluntates meas.

16. James Harvey Robinson, Readings in Modern European History, vol. 2 (Boston: Ginn, 1906), 509.

17. Ibid., 510.

18. Scholars generally agree that the speeches by Paul and others in Acts are not verbatim quotations, but rather free compositions by Luke, the author of Acts, who was adopting a literary convention of other biblical and nonbiblical historians.

19. See for example Joel Baden, The Historical David: The Real Life of an Invented Hero (New York: HarperOne, 2013).

20. 1 Samuel 17; 2 Samuel 21:19.

21. 1 Samuel 18:7–8.

22. 1 Samuel 24; 26.

23. 2 Samuel 1:19–27.

24. The stories of David's early life as a sheepherder (1 Samuel 16:11; 17:15, 28, 34–35, 40) may be a literary trope: the shepherd of sheep becomes a shepherd of a new flock. This is developed in Psalm 78:70–72.

25. Rahab (not to be confused with the prostitute of Jericho in Joshua 2, whose name is spelled differently in Hebrew) is one of the names for the primeval chaos monster; see Isaiah 51:9; Job 9:13. It is also used metaphorically for Egypt; see Isaiah 30:7; Psalm 87:4.

26. 1 Samuel 16:10; 17:12. According to 1 Chronicles 2:15, David was the seventh son of Jesse, not the eighth.

27. See Joshua 15:63; Judges 19:10–12.

28. 2 Samuel 6.

29. Asherah: a pole or stylized tree named for a Canaanite mother goddess. Baal: the Canaanite storm god.

30. Notably, in the Assyrian invasion in 701 and the first Babylonian campaign in 597 BCE.

31. Sometimes less correctly spelled Nebuchadnezzar; he ruled 605–562 BCE.

32. See Jeremiah 25:1–11.

33. The ark of the covenant, on which Yahweh was invisibly enthroned, had been located at Shiloh in the eleventh century BCE, but that did not prevent the city's destruction and the ark's capture by Israel's enemies the Philistines.

34. Genesis 18:19; see above, chapter 2, note 1.

35. Isaiah 10:5–6.

36. In the Bible, the land of Cush can mean either Midian, in southern Jordan and northern Saudi Arabia, or modern Sudan and Ethiopia, which is more likely in this period. Caphtor refers to Crete. Aram was a group of kingdoms in western Syria. The location of Kir is unknown (see also Amos 1:5; 2 Kings 16:9), and we have no evidence of an Aramean migration from anywhere.

37. "Teaching," Hebrew *torah.*

38. This passage, which is also found in Micah 4:1–2, is probably later than the time of Isaiah of Jerusalem, the late eighth century BCE, but it is still evidence for a more universalistic attitude. For similar sentiments, see Isaiah 45:14; 49:6; 51:4; 56:7; 60:3.

CHAPTER 5: WHICH SURVIVORS WERE CHOSEN?

1. It must have been hard to have a prophet for a father. Another of Isaiah's sons is named Maher-shalal-hash-baz ("Quickly the plunder, hastily the spoils"), also referring to the imminent Assyrian invasion; a third is named Immanuel ("God is with us") a perfectly ordinary name but also a vehicle for the prophet's message. Similarly, Hosea named two of his children Lo-ruhamah ("Not pitied") and Lo-ammi ("Not my people"); his firstborn, Jezreel ("God sows") again has an ordinary name but also one containing a prophetic proclamation.

2. See also Exodus 20:5–6; Numbers 14:18; Deuteronomy 5:9–10; Nehemiah 9:17, 31; Psalms 86:15; 103:8–9, 17; 145:8; Jeremiah 32:18; Joel 2:13; Jonah 4:2; Nahum 1:3; Daniel 9:4.

3. Ezekiel 11:14–15.

4. Ezekiel 10–11.

5. The metaphor of the good and bad figs is resumed in Jeremiah 29:16–19.

6. Although Maimonides's list of the 613 commandments found in the Hebrew Bible does not include the requirement of living in the Promised

Land, for many Zionists those Jews living in the Diaspora are not fully and authentically Jewish. Well over half of the Jews in the world live outside Israel, and for many of them, such a view is offensive.

7. Determining which parts of the book of Jeremiah go back to the prophet himself is difficult, but for our purposes here the issue is irrelevant: in either case, the passage shows that the notion of an empty land preceded its use by the authors of Chronicles.

8. This is from a section of Leviticus (chapters 17–26) known as the Holiness Code. Its date is disputed, but a majority of scholars date it to the exilic or postexilic period. The passage quoted seems to refer to the Babylonian exile.

9. See especially Exodus 23:10–11; also Leviticus 25:2–7. Deuteronomy 15:1–3 adds to the agricultural component a remission of debts every seven years, but that does not seem to be referred to here.

10. See also 1 Kings 9:7; Isaiah 6:11–12; 61:4; Ezekiel 36:10.

11. See Jeremiah 39:10.

12. See Jeremiah 52:28–30.

13. The text is in Hebrew. An expanded version of this decree is found in Ezra 1:2–4, in Aramaic, which was likely its original language.

14. See 2 Kings 17:24–28.

15. The fictional biblical book of Esther, which dates to the fourth or third century BCE, is entirely set in Persia, as is the court tale in Daniel 6, from about the same period.

16. The others are Miriam (Exodus 15:20), Deborah (Judges 4:4), and Huldah (2 Kings 22:14).

17. That is, Hebrew.

18. In the Hebrew version of Ezra (10:44) this expulsion is not clearly stated (the text is unclear), but it is found in a variant version, preserved in the Apocrypha in Greek (1 Esdras 9:36), and there is no good reason to doubt its authenticity.

19. Compare Exodus 2:21–22 with Numbers 12:1; note also the execution of a Midianite woman and her Israelite husband in Numbers 25:6–8.

20. See also Isaiah 2:2–4; Zechariah 2:11; 8:20–23; Malachi 1:11; all of these texts are from the postexilic period.

CHAPTER 6: CHRISTIANS AS A NEW CHOSEN PEOPLE

1. As is implied in John 4:20.

2. See John 4:9.

3. See Isaiah 40:3, quoted in Rule of the Community (1QS), VIII, 14.

4. The Commentary on Habakkuk Scroll (1QpHab), X, 13.

5. On the early Christian belief that the Second Coming was imminent, see, for example, Romans 13:11–12; 1 Corinthians 7:29; 1 Peter 4:7.

6. Galatians 2:12–14. For examples of Paul's self-identification, see 2 Corinthians 11:22 and Philippians 3:4–6.

7. In Acts 15:19–21, James is the leader of the Jerusalem church who as a compromise suggests that Gentile Christians do not need to observe all the requirements of the Torah; circumcision is not mentioned. This is likely an effort by Luke, the author of Acts, written several decades later, to paper over the sharp disagreements among early Christians.

8. This sentence is also found in a variant form in Luke 16:17, so scholars think that it belongs to an earlier hypothetical stage in the formation of the Gospels (known as Q), a collection of sayings attributed to Jesus dating to about the same time as Paul's letter to the Galatians.

9. This is the traditional understanding. More recently, scholars have suggested that it should be translated as "the faith of Jesus," that is, Gentiles attain righteousness because of Jesus's own faith in God. But perhaps the ambiguity is deliberate.

10. Romans 11:24; 10:12; Galatians 3:28.

11. Galatians 5:12.

12. See especially Isaiah 5:1–7; other examples include Isaiah 27:2–11 and Psalm 80:8–18.

13. See Mark 11:27.

14. A possibly earlier expression of the same view is in 1 Thessalonians 2:14–16:

> For, brothers, you became imitators of the churches of God that are in Judea in Christ Jesus, for you suffered the same things from your own compatriots as they did from the Jews, who killed both the Lord Jesus and the prophets, and drove us out, and they are not pleasing to God and oppose everyone, preventing us from speaking to the Gentiles so that they may be saved, to constantly fill up the measure of their sins. The wrath has finally come upon them.

Although there is no textual basis for considering these verses a later addition, many scholars do so, because the thoughts expressed are inconsistent with Paul's views elsewhere (summarized above). The last few words may also allude to the destruction of Jerusalem in 70 CE, which occurred some two decades after this letter was written, and after Paul's death. On the other hand, the term "Jews" may refer only to the Judean leaders (see pages 82–83); in this case the passage is not as overly anti-Jewish as it seems, and could be from Paul, whose own thinking was not always consistent, especially as it evolved.

15. Although capital punishment was prescribed in biblical law, in the first century CE the Romans did not allow Jewish religious authorities to enforce it, reserving that prerogative for themselves.

16. The texts are quoted from the Septuagint, the ancient translation of the Hebrew Bible into Greek, which the New Testament writers, who wrote in Greek, generally used. Although the original Hebrew of Isaiah 43:20 has "people," the Septuagint uses *genos*, which I translate as "group"; the usual

translation as "race" is potentially misleading. "Royal priesthood" is the Septuagint's translation of the Hebrew, which literally means "kingdom of priests." See further discussion on page 38.

17. The same claim, using some of the same language, is also found in Revelation 1:6; 5:10.

18. For Luke's appearances in the New Testament, see Colossians 4:14; 2 Timothy 4:11; Philemon 24.

19. This also explains some changes in the arrangement of parts of the canon. In Judaism, the order was (and is) Torah, (Former and Latter) Prophets, and Writings, but in Christianity the (Latter) Prophets (Isaiah through Malachi) were (and are) put last, just before the Gospel accounts of Jesus's life, teaching, death, and resurrection, which they were interpreted as predicting.

20. No such a pardon at Passover is attested elsewhere.

21. See Matthew 4:23 (parallels in Mark 1:39; Luke 4:44); 9:35; 12:9 (Mark 3:1; Luke 6:6); 13:54 (Mark 6:2; Luke 4:16); Mark 1:21 (Luke 4:31); Luke 4:15; 13:10; John 6:59; 18:20.

22. See also John 9:22; 16:2. Other Gospels speak of believers being flogged in the synagogue, but not literally expelled (Matthew 10:17 [Mark 13:9; Luke 21:12]; 23:34).

23. For examples of transgenerational punishment, see Genesis 3:19; Exodus 20:5. See also above, page 62.

24. For the Samaritan woman's remark to Jesus, see John 4:22.

25. In his *Dialogue with Trypho*, the second-century Christian apologist Justin Martyr tells his Jewish interlocutor that "your scriptures are not yours, but ours" (29), and that "we are the true Israelites" (135).

26. "Oremus et pro perfidis Judaeis: ut Deus et Dominus noster auferat velamen de cordibus eorum; ut et ipsi agnoscant Jesus Christum, Dominum nostrum. Omnipotens sempiterne Deus, qui etiam judaicam perfidiam a tua misericordia non repellis: exaudi preces nostras, quas pro illius populi obcaecatione deferimus; ut, agnita veritatis tuae luce, que Christus est, a suis tenebris eruantur"; *Missale Romanum ex Decreto Concilii Tridentini Restitutum* (Bonnae ad Rhenum: Aedibus Palmarum, 2004), 221–22 (available at musicasacra.com/pdf/romanmissal_classical.pdf). In 1959, Pope John XXIII removed the word *perfidis* ("perfidious"), but the rest was unchanged. For the current English version (2011), see page 86.

27. "The Lenten Triodion," Holy Week, Friday, Matins: http://www.ocf .org/OrthodoxPage/prayers/triodion/triodion.html, 6–7.

28. *The Book of Common Prayer from the Original Manuscript Attached to the Act of Uniformity of 1662 and Now Preserved in the House of Lords* (London: Eyre & Spottiswood [1892]), 145. I have modernized the spelling.

29. *The Roman Missal: English Translation According to the Third Typical Edition* (Chicago: Archdiocese of Chicago, Liturgy Training Publications, 2011), 323. But the revived Latin liturgy for Good Friday, has this revision

of the original, made by Pope Benedict XVI in 2008, which returns to a
more explicit supersessionism: "Oremus et pro Iudaeis: Ut Deus et Dominus
noster illuminet corda eorum, ut agnoscant Iesum Christum salvatorem
omnium hominum. . . . Omnipotens sempiterne Deus, qui vis ut omnes
homines salvi fiant et ad agnitionem veritatis veniant, concede propitius,
ut plenitudine gentium in Ecclesiam Tuam intrante omnis Israel salvus fiat"
(*L'Osservatore Romano*, February 6, 2008); "Let us also pray for the Jews:
That our God and Lord may illuminate their hearts, that they recognize
that Jesus Christ is the Savior of all men. . . . Almighty, eternal God, who
wishes that all men be saved and come to the recognition of the truth,
propitiously grant that as the fullness of peoples enters Thy Church, all
Israel be saved."

30. Krister Stendahl, "Anti-Semitism," in *The Oxford Companion to the Bible*, ed. B. M. Metzger and M. D. Coogan (New York: Oxford University Press, 1993), 33. The term "anti-Semitism" is, etymologically at least, inaccurate, since the Semites include not just Jews but Arabs, Ethiopians, and others. Some scholars prefer the more precise term "anti-Judaism," but here I follow standard usage.

CHAPTER 7: BEYOND THE BIBLE

1. See John 19:36, referring to Exodus 12:46; Numbers 9:12; see also John 1:29; Revelation 5:12.

2. "God . . . caused the children of Abraham to pass dry-shod through the Red Sea, so that the chosen people, set free from slavery to Pharaoh, would prefigure the people of the baptized," *The Roman Missal: English Translation According to the Third Typical Edition* (Chicago: Archdiocese of Chicago, Liturgy Training Publications, 2011), 377.

3. "Allah" is simply the Arabic word for God, not the name of a different deity. When Arab Christians pray, they address God as "Allah." So, the god of Islam is identical with the god of Judaism and Christianity.

4. Later, Muslim scholars will argue that the Jewish and Christian sacred scriptures have been corrupted (this is the doctrine of *tahrif*), so that the only reliable version of the Jewish and Christian scriptures is that found in the Qur'an itself.

5. Interestingly, the Church of Jesus Christ of Latter Day Saints, the Mormons, have a parallel view: the Book of Mormon is the final and definitive revelation, building on but not replacing the Old and New Testaments.

6. Matthew 1:1–17; Luke 3:23–34.

7. See, for example, Romans 4:16–22; Hebrews 11:8–19.

8. Tarif Khalidi, trans., *The Qur'an* (New York: Penguin, 2008), 48.

9. See 2 Samuel 24:18–25; 2 Chronicles 3:1.

10. See, for example, Isaiah 52:1; Nehemiah 11:1; 1 Maccabees 2:7; Matthew 4:5.

11. 2 Chronicles 3:1; Genesis 22:2, 14.

12. The Qur'an does not name the son whom God told Abraham to sacrifice, but later Muslim traditions identify him as Ishmael.

13. The precise phrase "holy land" is used only once in the Hebrew Bible, in Zechariah 2:12; see also 2 Maccabees 1:7; Wisdom of Solomon 12:3. It is not used in the New Testament. For "holy city," see Revelation 11:2; 21:2.

14. East of the Temple Mount, on the Mount of Olives, is the Chapel of the Ascension, which also has an indentation identified as Jesus's footprint as he ascended to heaven. Reputed footprints of other religious notables such as Adam and the Buddha as well as of many gods and goddesses are found all over the world.

15. For Judaism and Christianity, see pages 118–20. For Islam, see "A Common Word Between Us and You," A Common Word, https://www.acommonword.com/the-acw-document, accessed August 24, 2018.

16. For a survey of Western examples of national self-identification as being divinely chosen, see W. R. Hutchison and H. Lehmann, eds., *Many Are Chosen: Divine Election and Western Nationalism*, Harvard Theological Studies 38 (Minneapolis: Fortress, 1974).

CHAPTER 8: GOD SHED HIS LIGHT ON THEE?

1. The exact phrasing was popularized by Conrad Cherry in the anthology he edited, *God's New Israel: Religious Interpretations of American Destiny*, rev. ed. (Chapel Hill: University of North Carolina Press, 1998), title and page 21, but the underlying concept is widespread, as Cherry's important collection shows. Ezra Stiles uses the phrase "God's American Israel" in "The United States Elevated to Glory and Honor (1783)," ed. Reiner Smolinski, *Electronic Texts in American Studies* 41 (http://digital commons.unl.edu/etas/41), 7, 36.

2. Throughout this chapter I have modernized spelling and punctuation.

3. *Bradford's History of "Plimoth Plantation," from the Original Manuscript* (Boston: Wright and Potter, 1899), 96–97, available at http://www.gutenberg.org/files/24950/24950-h/24950-h.htm.

4. We find nothing like this self-identification in Canada, which has been called "a country without a mythology," the title of a poem by the Canadian poet Douglas LePan. See also, for example, Sacvan Bercovitch, *The American Jeremiad* (Madison: University of Wisconsin Press, 1979), 11.

5. Still, Cotton himself immigrated to New England in 1633, fearing for his safety because of his nonconformity.

6. John Cotton, "God's Promise to His Plantation (1630)," ed. Reiner Smolinski, *Electronic Texts in American Studies* 22, http://digitalcommons.unl.edu/etas/22, 3.

7. Cotton, "God's Promise," "Preface to the Christian Reader."

8. Cotton, "God's Promise," 20.

9. Some of these are no longer in use. For a fuller, although incomplete discussion, see John Leighly, "Biblical Place-Names in the United States,"

Names 27 (1979): 46–59. Also incomplete, and less reliable, are Abraham I. Katsh, "Place Names of Biblical or Hebrew Origin," in *The Biblical Heritage of American Democracy* (New York: Ktav, 1977), 169–72 and inset map; and Moshe Davis, "Biblical Place Names in America," in *America and the Holy Land* (Westport, CT: Praeger, 1995), 135–45.

10. *The Danger of Desertion* (London: Printed by G. M. for George Edwards in the Old Baily in Greene-Arbour, at the signe of the Angell, 1641), 15; compare Ezekiel 11:23, and see page 63.

11. Ibid., "Epistle to the Reader," 2.

12. *An Apology of the Churches in New England for Church Covenant* (London: Printed by T. P. and M. S. for Benjamin Allen, 1643), 1, available at http://quod.lib.umich.edu/e/eebo/A50245.0001.001?rgn=main;view =fulltext.

13. For a summary of the issues of timing, see Francis J. Bremer, *John Winthrop: America's Forgotten Founding Father* (New York: Oxford University Press, 2003), 174–75, 431–32. The published version of the sermon published in 1838 states that it was "written on board the *Arbella*, on the Atlantic Ocean."

14. "*Beloved there is now set before us life and good, death and evil, in that we are commanded this day to love the Lord our God, and to love one another, to walk in his ways and to keep his commandments and his ordinance and his laws,* and the articles of our covenant with him, *that we may live and be multiplied, and that the Lord may bless us in the land whither we go to possess it. But if our hearts shall turn away, so that we will not obey, but shall be seduced, and worship and serve other gods,* our pleasures and profits, *and serve them,* it is propounded unto us this day, *we shall surely perish out of the good land whither we pass over this vast sea to possess it;* therefore let us choose life that we and our seed may live, by obeying his voice and cleaving to him, for he is our life and prosperity," John Winthrop, *A Modell of Christian Charity* (*1630*), Collections of the Massachusetts Historical Society (Boston: 1838), 47–48 (available at http://history.hanover.edu/texts/winthmod.html); italics, indicating quotation from the Bible, are in the original, but even more of this section is from Deuteronomy 30 than is in italics.

15. Winthrop, *Modell of Christian Charity*, 47.

16. Samuel Wakeman, *Sound repentance the right way to escape deserved ruine; or A solid and awakening discourse, exhorting the people of God to comply with his counsel, by a hearty practical turning from sin to himself and his service thereby to prevent their being made desolate by his departing from them. As it was delivered in a sermon preached at Hartford on Connecticut in New England, May 14th. 1685. Being the day of election there*, page 18 (available at http://quod.lib. umich.edu/e/evans/N00324.0001.001/1:3?rgn=div1;view=fulltext).

17. He estimated that the millennium would begin in some seven hundred or eight hundred years.

18. Stiles, "The United States Elevated to Glory and Honor," 56.

19. See Psalm 80:14 and page 76.

20. Stiles, "The United States Elevated to Glory and Honor," 35.

21. Ibid., 37–39, 43.

22. Ibid., 44; see Numbers 21:14.

23. Ibid., 52–53 (quoted from a letter of Adams dated December 18, 1781).

24. The phrase was coined by Rousseau; its application to the United States was famously made by Robert N. Bellah, "Civil Religion in America," *Daedalus* 96 (1967): 1–21.

25. Proposal for the Great Seal of the United States, Founders Online, National Archives, https://founders.archives.gov/documents/Franklin/01-22-02-0330, accessed August 23, 2018.

26. "Common Sense," *The Writings of Thomas Paine*, vol. 1, ed. M. D. Conway (New York: G. P. Putnam's Sons, 1894), 93. In the same pamphlet, Paine also highlights the antimonarchical views in Judges (8:22–23) and 1 Samuel (8; 12) as evidence that "monarchy is ranked in scripture as one of the sins of the Jews, for which a curse in reserve is denounced against them" ("Common Sense," 76). He thus dismisses establishment of the monarchy in Israel as human error rather than divine choice, considering authoritative only the biblical texts that support his republican views.

27. "Annexation," *The United States Magazine and Democratic Review* 17, no. 1 (July/August 1845): 5.

28. Herman Melville, *White Jacket, or The World in a Man-of-War*, orig. 1850 (New York: Quality Paperback Club, 1996), 189, http://www.gutenberg.org/files/10712/10712-h/10712-h.htm.

29. *Harper's New Monthly Magazine* 17, no. 101 (October 1858): 694, 699–700.

30. Exodus 3:5; Joshua 5:15.

31. A. A. Lipscomb, *Our Country: Its Danger and Duty* (New York: American Protestant Society, 1844), 85, 101, 120.

32. "March of the Flag": Speech by Hon. Albert J. Beveridge, Opening the Campaign of 1898, Delivered at Tomlinson Hall, September 16, Indianapolis, Ind., 2; available at https://archive.org/stream/marchofflagbeginoobeve#page/no/mode/2up.

33. Ibid., 16.

34. See David Domke and Kevin Coe, *The God Strategy: How Religion Became a Political Weapon in America*, updated ed. (New York: Oxford University Press, 2010), 45. As they point out, the phrase was earlier used by President Nixon in a speech during the Watergate crisis.

35. For example, see Reagan's acceptance speech at the Republican National Convention, Dallas, Texas, August 23, 1984, https://www.reaganlibrary.gov/research/speeches/82384f; Ronald Reagan, Farewell

Address, January 11, 1989,https://www.reaganfoundation.org/media/128652
/farewell.pdf.
36. George W. Bush, President's Remarks to the Nation, Ellis Island,
September 11, 2012, https://georgewbush-whitehouse.archives.gov/news
/releases/2002/09/20020911-3.html.
37. See also John 8:12.
38. In a letter of May 28, 1664, to the younger John Winthrop, in J. R.
Bartlett, ed., *The Complete Writings of Roger Williams*, vol. 6, *Letters of Roger
Williams* (New York: Russell & Russell, 1963), 319.
39. Abraham Lincoln, Address to the New Jersey State Senate, February 21, 1861, available at http://www.abrahamlincolnonline.org/lincoln
/speeches/trenton1.htm.

CHAPTER 9: FUNDAMENTALIST ZIONISMS

1. Estimating population especially during the Ottoman period is difficult and sometimes controversial; see David Grossman, "Arab Population
in Palestine During the Ottoman Era: Perceptions and Reality," *Horizons in
Geography* 79/80 (2012): 136–53. Sources I have used include "The Population of Palestine Prior to 1948" (2002–2007), http://www.mideastweb
.org/palpop.htm, and Sergio DellaPergola, "Demography in Israel/Palestine:
Trends, Prospects, Policy Implications," IUSSP XXIV General Population
Conference, Salvador de Bahia, August 2001, http://fc.retecivica.mi.it
/rcmweb/testwebisraele/Israele/Aliyah%20e%20diaspora/Demografia%20e
%20sviluppo/S03DoF4A4.0/Demography%20in%20IsraelPalesti.pdf. All
numbers have been rounded off. Some of the overall increase was due to
natural population growth, but immigration was the reason for the significantly greater increase of the Jewish population.
2. The exact Hebrew of the last words—*ge'ullat yisra'el*—is not biblical,
but was a motto on coins of the Second Jewish Revolt (132–35 CE), the
previous incarnation of an independent Jewish state. The language of God
redeeming Israel, however, occurs often in the Bible.
3. Some ultraconservative Hasidic sects, such as the Satmar Hasidim,
opposed Zionism, and claimed that the Holocaust was divine punishment
for attempting to restore Israel before the coming of the Messiah.
4. Israeli political parties, like those in Italy and France, change
frequently.
5. Quoted in Yehoshafat Harkabi, *Israel's Fateful Hour*, trans. Lenn
Schramm (New York: Harper & Row, 1988), 145.
6. See pages 55–56.
7. Israel Shahak and Norton Mezvinsky, *Jewish Fundamentalism in
Israel*, 2d ed. (London: Pluto, 2004), 70.
8. For example, Meir Kahane: see Raphaël Mergui and Philippe Simon-
not, *Meïr Kahane: Le rabbin qui fait peur aux Juifs* (Lausanne: Pierre-Marcel
Favre, 1985), 51. See also Ian S. Lustick, *For the Land and the Lord: Jewish*

Fundamentalism in Israel (New York: Council on Foreign Relations, 1988), 36, 105–10; Nadav G. Shelef, *Evolving Nationalism: Homeland, Identity, and Religion in Israel, 1925–2005* (Ithaca, NY: Cornell University Press, 2010), 50–80.

9. In an interview with Walter Reich, recounted in his *A Stranger in My House: Jews and Arabs in the West Bank* (New York: Holt, Rinehart & Winston, 1984), 15.

10. See Moshe Weinfeld, *The Promise of the Land: The Inheritance of the Land of Canaan by the Israelites* (Berkeley: University of California Press, 1993), chap. 3, "The Borders of the Promised Land: Two Views."

11. In a demonstration against the Israeli government's (temporary) freeze on new construction in the West Bank settlements in 2009, protesters are shown carrying signs that read "God's Bible gave *us* this land," Aron Heller, "Settlers protest in Jerusalem against construction freeze," *Boston Globe*, December 10, 2009, A24.

12. Ultrareligious Zionists also refer to Palestinian Arabs as "Amalekites," traditional enemies of the Israelites during the Exodus period, and as "Canaanites," the original inhabitants of the Promised Land; both are groups that Yahweh reportedly commanded the Israelites to annihilate.

13. Genesis 25:13–15.

14. Marc Haber et al., "Continuity and Admixture in the Last Five Millennia of Levantine History from Ancient Canaanite and Present-Day Lebanese Genome Sequences," *American Journal of Human Genetics* 101 (August 3, 2017): 1; see also Nicholas St. Fleur, "Fate of Ancient Canaanites Seen in DNA Analysis: They Survived," *New York Times*, July 27, 2017, https://www.nytimes.com/2017/07/27/science/ancient-canaanites-bible-lebanon.html.

15. Quoted in Michael Karpin and Ina Friedman, *Murder in the Name of God: The Plot to Kill Yitzhak Rabin* (New York: Metropolitan, 1998), 39–40; see also Lustick, *For the Land and the Lord*, 30–37.

16. Quoted in Lustick, *For the Land and the Lord*, 82–83.

17. See, for example, Brian Klug, "A Time to Move On," in *A Time to Speak Out: Independent Jewish Voices on Israel, Zionism, and Jewish Identity*, ed. A. Karpf et al. (London: Verso, 2008), 293. Opposition to some Israeli government policies by non-Jews is not necessarily anti-Semitic, any more so than when it is expressed by Jews, both Israelis and in the Diaspora.

18. Harold Fisch, *The Zionist Revolution: A New Perspective* (New York: St. Martin's, 1978), 77–78.

19. Not coincidentally, Christian Zionism developed in tandem with European Jewish Zionism. For an overview, see Ruth Mouly and Roland Robertson, "Zionism in American Premillenarian Fundamentalism," *American Journal of Theology and Philosophy* 4, no. 3 (September 1983): 97–109, and see also Victoria Clark, *Allies for Armageddon: The Rise of Christian Zionism* (New Haven, CT: Yale University Press, 2007).

20. The lovely American Colony Hotel was once part of the group's estate. The German Colony, another Jerusalem neighborhood, has similar millenarian origins.

21. See also Isaiah 11:11–16; Jeremiah 32:37, 33:7–9; Ezekiel 20:41–42; Zechariah 12:6, 9; etc.

22. See Paul Boyer, *When Time Shall Be No More: Prophecy Belief in Modern American Culture* (Cambridge, MA: Harvard University Press, 1992), 187–224.

23. John Hagee, *Four Blood Moons: Something Is About to Change* (Brentwood, TN: Worthy, 2013), 244.

24. Compare 1 Thessalonians 4:13–18.

25. Some scholars think that different authors are responsible for different numbers, but that of course would undermine the supposed divine authority of the text.

26. Revelation 22:12; see also 1 Thessalonians 4:15–17, in which Paul expects that Jesus's return will be during his lifetime, because, as he says in 1 Corinthians 7:29, "the time has grown short." See further page 143n5.

27. The last phrase can also be translated positively: Ishmael will live "alongside all his brothers."

CHAPTER 10: IMMIGRANTS AND REFUGEES, IDEALS AND REALITIES

1. Genesis 23:4; see also Genesis 35:27; Exodus 6:4; Psalm 105:12. The Common English Bible often translates *ger* as "immigrant." The King James Version generally uses "sojourner" or "stranger"; the New Jewish Publication Society translation uses "stranger," "resident alien," and "sojourner"; the New Revised Standard Version uses both "alien" (which smacks of extraterrestrials) and "resident alien," as well as "stranger." In Genesis 23:4, Abraham also calls himself a *toshab*, a relatively rare word roughly synonymous with *ger*, and sometimes, as here, used in conjunction with it to form a hendiadys.

2. Genesis 12:10–13:1.

3. For the Israelites' status as "temporary residents" in Egypt, see Genesis 15:13; Exodus 2:22; 18:3.

4. "Native-born" corresponds to Hebrew *ezrah*.

5. See especially Exodus 20:16–17 and Deuteronomy 5:20–21; see further Michael Coogan, *The Ten Commandments: A Short History of an Ancient Text* (New Haven, CT: Yale University Press, 2014), 88–89.

6. Israelites who left their own tribal territory and moved to another tribe's territory were also considered immigrants, as were those who moved to another country; see Judges 19:16; Ruth 1:1; 2 Samuel 4:3.

7. "An eye for an eye": Leviticus 24:17–22 (and see also Exodus 12:49; Numbers 15:16; Deuteronomy 1:16; Joshua 20:9); Sabbath: Exodus 20:10; Deuteronomy 5:14; purity: Leviticus 17:10–13; 18:26; but see Deuteronomy 14:21; blasphemy: Leviticus 24:16.

8. Passover: Exodus 12:48; Numbers 9:14; festival of Weeks: Deuteronomy 16:11; festival of Booths: Deuteronomy 16:14; Day of Atonement: Leviticus 16:29. See also Numbers 19:10; Joshua 8:33, 35.

9. But see Ezekiel 47:21–23.

10. Leviticus 25:45–46.

11. Ruth is an exception; although she calls herself a foreigner (Ruth 2:10), she had already committed to living in Bethlehem with Naomi (Ruth 1:16–17).

12. Note the foreign origin of mercenaries such as Doeg the Edomite (1 Samuel 22:9); Uriah the Hittite (2 Samuel 11; 23:39); Ittai the Gittite (that is, from Gath; 2 Samuel 15:19); and the royal bodyguard, the Cherethites (Cretans) and the Pelethites, who were perhaps Philistines, like the Gittites (2 Samuel 8:18; 15:18; 1 Kings 1:38); these men may have intended to return to their own territories. Note also the use of "Canaanite" to mean "merchant" (Zechariah 14:21; Proverbs 31:24; see also Hosea 12:7; Zephaniah 1:11).

13. Deuteronomy 23:20.

14. 1 Samuel 8:14.

15. Leviticus 25:44–46.

16. For prisoners of war, see, for example, Numbers 31:15–18; Deuteronomy 21:10–14; 2 Chronicles 28:8–10. For children, see Exodus 21:4.

17. See, for example, Genesis 12:16; 20:14; 24:35; Exodus 20:17; Deuteronomy 5:21.

18. See Genesis 17:12; Exodus 12:44.

19. Deuteronomy 5:14–15; see also Exodus 23:12. The version of the Sabbath commandment in Exodus 20:11 gives a different reason: the Israelites are to rest in imitation of the divine rest on the seventh day after the six days of creation (see Genesis 2:2–3).

20. See, for example, Leviticus 25:39–42, 55; NRSV "they are my servants," literally "they are my slaves."

21. See Exodus 21:2–6.

22. In Hebrew, golah, galut, and cognates.

23. In Hebrew, palit and cognates.

24. Deuteronomy 23:15–16.

25. See Numbers 35:6–34; Deuteronomy 4:41–43; 19:1–10; Joshua 20:3–9; 21:13–39.

26. See Exodus 22:21–22; Deuteronomy 14:29; 24:17–22; Jeremiah 7:6; 22:3; Ezekiel 22:7; Zechariah 7:10; Malachi 3:5; Psalms 94:6; 146:9; Job 31:16–22, 32.

27. The exception most often cited is Laws of Eshnunna 41, but its interpretation is far from clear.

28. The Greek for "stranger" is xenos. In the Septuagint, the ancient translation of the Hebrew Bible into Greek, xenos translates the Hebrew words for both immigrant (ger) and foreigner (nokri). A xenos, like a ger, was

an outsider, often although not necessarily a foreigner, with whom the host had a relationship that is often translated as "guest-friendship." An epithet of Zeus is *xe(i)nios*, which means approximately protector of guests/strangers; see *Odyssey* 9.266–70, and compare Leviticus 25:23; Psalm 39:12. I think that in Matthew 25:35, 38, the author likely means both immigrant and foreigner.

29. According to the Jesus Seminar, this parable is something that Jesus undoubtedly said; see Robert W. Funk, Roy W. Hoover, and the Jesus Seminar, *The Five Gospels: The Search for the Authentic Words of Jesus* (New York: Macmillan, 1993), 323–24.

30. Deuteronomy does not have "with all your mind." In Matthew 22:35–49 and Mark 12:29–31, Jesus himself gives this answer.

31. The usual Christian explanation is that they wanted to avoid ritual impurity through contact with what they thought was a corpse. But the parable does not state that, and, as Amy-Jill Levine notes, ritual purity is not a concern of Luke's here. Rather, she suggests, these members of the religious establishment are singled out for failing to do what they should— that is, to save a life (Amy-Jill Levine, *Short Stories by Jesus: The Enigmatic Parables of a Controversial Rabbi* [New York: HarperOne, 2015], 99–102).

32. For example, John 4:9; 8:48; Josephus, *Antiquities* 20.118–36.

33. See Robert W. Funk, Roy W. Hoover, and the Jesus Seminar, *The Five Gospels*, 147. The saying is found in different contexts in the two Gospels, suggesting that it was an originally independent saying likely belonging to the earliest stage of the Jesus tradition. In Matthew, it occurs in the Sermon on the Mount, in a section in which Jesus, as a kind of new Moses, contrasts his teaching with that of the Torah. He introduces each topic with a quotation from the Torah. Here he proclaims, "You have heard that it was said, 'You should love your neighbor and hate your enemy.' But I say to you, 'Love your enemies'" (5:43–44). "Love your neighbor" is a quotation of Leviticus 19:18, but "hate your enemy" is not found in the Hebrew Bible. Luke's variant of the Sermon on the Mount, the "sermon on the plain" (see Luke 6:17), repeats the command in 6:35.

34. Interestingly, in the variant of this law in Deuteronomy 22:1–4, it is the "brother's" (NRSV "neighbor's") straying animals that are to be returned.

35. The following verse ("For you will heap burning coals on his head, and Yahweh will reward you") is obscure.

36. Virtually the same view is attributed to Rabbi Akiba in Sifra Qedoshim 4.12: "'Love your neighbor as yourself' . . . is the greatest principle in the Torah." See also Romans 13:8–10; Galatians 5:14; and see further Matthew 5:39–42 and Luke 6:29–31, also "red-letter sayings" of Jesus according to the Jesus Seminar.

37. Deuteronomy 20:10–17.

38. Judges 1:27–36; see also 1 Kings 9:20–21.

39. Abraham: Genesis 12:16; 17:23; Jacob: Genesis 30:43; Solomon: 1 Kings 9:21; Job: Job 31:13; the returnees: Nehemiah 7:66–67.

40. 1 Peter 2:18.

41. This is the popular version; the texts literally say, "And as you wish that people do to you, you should do similarly to them" (Luke 6:31) and "Everything that you wish that people do to you, so you should do to them" (Matthew 7:12).

42. Prior to this date, several Marrano Jewish families had been living in London for some time.

43. Esther Meir-Glitzenstein, *Zionism in an Arab Country: Jews in Iraq in the 1940s* (London: Routledge, 2004), xi.

44. Norman A. Stillman, *The Jews of Arab Lands in Modern Times* (Philadelphia: Jewish Publication Society, 1991), 157.

45. See Benny Morris, *The Birth of the Palestinian Refugee Problem, 1947–1949* (Cambridge, UK: Cambridge University Press, 1987), 204–11; and Ari Shavit, *My Promised Land: The Triumph and Tragedy of Israel* (New York: Spiegel & Grau, 2013), 106–30.

46. The fourth charge against Williams was "that a man ought not to give thanks . . . after meat" (John Winthrop, *Journal of John Winthrop*, ed. Richard Dunn, James Savage, and Laetitia Yeandle [Cambridge, MA: Belknap Press of Harvard University Press, 1995], 150).

47. Genesis 11:9.

48. Genesis 9:20–27. Although Ham is the guilty party (see page 20 in this book), Noah curses Ham's son Canaan.

49. Stiles, "The United States Elevated to Glory and Honor," 10. For a general discussion, of the origins of Native Americans, see Lee Eldridge Huddleston, *Origins of the American Indians: European Concepts, 1492–1729* (Austin: University of Texas Press, 1967).

50. The same theory had been proposed by Spanish explorers of the Western Hemisphere; see Tudor Parfitt, *The Lost Tribes of Israel: The History of a Myth* (London: Phoenix, 2003 [2002]), 34–40.

51. The texts include Isaiah 27:13, Ezekiel 37:21, and Romans 11:25–27.

52. Quoted without a reference by Cotton Mather, in his *Magnalia Christi Americana, or, The Ecclesiastical History of New England, from Its First Planting, in the Year 1620, unto the Year of Our Lord 1698*, book 3 (Hartford, CT: S. Andrus & Son, 1853 [1702]), 160. Other notables who held the same view were William Penn: see M. L. Weems, *The Wife of William Penn* (Philadelphia: Uriah Hunt, 1829), 174; and Thomas Thorowgood: see Richard W. Cogley, "The Ancestry of the American Indians: Thomas Thorowgood's *Iewes in America* (1650) and *Jews in America* (1660)," *English Literary Renaissance* 35 (2005): 304–30.

53. *A Key into the Language of America, or An help to the Language of the Natives in that part of America, called New-England* (London: Gregory

Dexter, 1643; reprint Providence, RI: Rhode Island and Providence Plantations Tercentenary Committee, 1936), 53.

54. For example, 2 Nephi 1.9; 30.4. See also Simon G. Southerton, *Losing a Lost Tribe: Native Americans, DNA, and the Mormon Church* (Salt Lake City: Signature Books, 2004).

55. "The Song Millennial," https://www.loc.gov/resource/amss.as112790.0 /?st=text.

56. "Letter to Martin Van Buren, President of the United States," in *The Portable Emerson*, ed. Carl Bode in collaboration with Malcolm Cowley, new ed. (New York: Penguin, 1981), 530, 527–28.

57. Jim Wallis made this claim of original sin, first in *Sojourners* November 1987 (https://sojo.net/magazine/november-1987/americas-original-sin); see also his *America's Original Sin: Racism, White Privilege, and the Bridge to a New America* (Grand Rapids, MI: Brazos, 2016). Even the Declaration of Independence has a racist cast; note this complaint against King George III: "He has excited domestic insurrections among us, and has endeavoured to bring on the inhabitants of our frontiers, the merciless Indian Savages whose known rule of warfare, is an undistinguished destruction of all ages, sexes, and conditions." In his speech "A More Perfect Union," on March 18, 2008, then Senator Barack Obama called slavery "this nation's original sin" (http://obamaspeeches.com/E05-Barack-Obama-A-More-Perfect-Union-the -Race-Speech-Philadelphia-PA-March-18-2008.htm).

58. US Bureau of the Census, *Statistical Abstract of the United States: 1957*, 78th ed. (Washington, DC: 1957), 94.

59. For the United States as a whole, see https://www.census.gov/content /dam/Census/newsroom/releases/2015/cb15-tps16_graphic.pdf. For individual cities, see www.diversitydata.org.

60. Gabriel J. Chin and Rose Cuison Villazor, "Introduction," *The Immigration and Nationality Act of 1965: Legislating a New America*, ed. G. J. Chin and R. C. Villazor (New York: Cambridge University Press, 2015), 2. For removal statistics, see https://www.ice.gov/removal-statistics/2016.

61. In a letter to her sister Edith (September 6, 1876), Ellen Tucker Emerson, Ralph Waldo Emerson's daughter, wrote after Lazarus's visit to Concord: "She has been brought up to keep the Law, and the Feast of the Passover, and the Day of Atonement. . . . She says her family are outlawed now, they no longer keep the Law" (Edith E. W. Gregg, ed., *The Letters of Ellen Tucker Emerson* [Kent, OH: Kent State University Press, 1982], 2:225).

62. Emma Lazarus, *An Epistle to the Hebrews*, centennial ed., with introduction and notes by Morris U. Schappes (New York: Jewish Historical Society of New York, 1987 [1890]), 57, 44, 38, 36. These essays were first published in *The American Hebrew* in 1882 and 1883.

63. UNHCR, Figures at a Glance, http://www.unhcr.org/en-us/figures -at-a-glance.html, accessed June 20, 2018.

64. UNHCR, Resettlement Data, January–June 2018, http://www.unhcr
.org/en-us/resettlement-data.html.

65. See "Summary of Refugee Admissions," Bureau of Population, Refugees, and Migration, December 31, 2015, https://2009-2017.state.gov/j/prm
/releases/statistics/251288.htm. For 2016, see Gardiner Harris, "U.S. Quietly
Lifts Limit on Number of Refugees Allowed In," *New York Times*, May 26,
2017, https://www.nytimes.com/2017/05/26/us/politics/united-states-refugees
-trump.html?_r=0.

66. International Rescue Committee, "How Many Refugees Are Resettled in the US and Who Decides?," Refugees in America, https://www
.rescue.org/topic/refugees-america#how-many-refugees-ae-resettled-in-the
-us-and-who-decides, accessed September 10, 2018.

CHAPTER 11: BEYOND TRIBALISM

1. "Gottes Reich and Deutsches Reich hatten ein Bund geschlos-
sen: 'Ich will dein Gott sein und du sollst mein Volk sein,'" *Der deutsche
Christusgemeinde: Der Weg zur deutschen Nationalkirche* (Weimar: Verlag
Deutsche Christen, 1935), 4; the translation here is by Mary M. Solberg,
*A Church Undone: Documents from the German Christian Faith Movement
1932–1940* (Minneapolis: Fortress, 2015), 325; compare Exodus 6:7; Leviti-
cus 26:12; etc. Leutheuser's colleague Siegfried Leffler similarly claimed that
Germany had been given a mission from God, and the leader and prophet
was Adolf Hitler, in *Christus in Dritten Reich der Deutschen: Wesen, Weg
Und Ziel der Kirchenbewegung "Deutsche Christen"* (Weimar: Verlag Deut-
sche Christen, [1935]), quoted in Robert P. Ericksen, *Theologians Under
Hitler: Gerhard Kittel, Paul Althaus and Emanuel Hirsch* (New Haven, CT:
Yale University Press, 1986), 90.

2. *New York Morning News*, December 27, 1845.

3. For a current example, see Steven E. Strang, *God and Donald Trump*
(Lake Mary, FL: Frontline, 2017).

4. On the US Constitution, note Justice Kennedy's words in *Obergefell
v. Hodges*, the decision that recognized a constitutional right to same-sex
marriage: "The nature of injustice is that we may not always see it in our
own times. The generations that wrote and ratified the Bill of Rights and
the Fourteenth Amendment did not presume to know the extent of freedom in all of its dimensions. . . . When new insight reveals discord between
the Constitution's central provisions and a received legal stricture, a claim
to liberty must be addressed" (135 S. Ct. 2584, 2598 [2015] at 11).

5. See further Michael Coogan, *God and Sex: What the Bible Really Says*
(New York: Twelve, 2010), 189–95.

6. Levine, *Short Stories by Jesus*, 114–15.

BIBLIOGRAPHY

Anderson, Bradford A. *Brotherhood and Inheritance: A Canonical Reading of the Esau and Edom Traditions.* New York: Bloomsbury, 2011.

Bercovitch, Sacvan. *The American Jeremiad.* Madison: University of Wisconsin Press, 1978.

Bergen, Doris L. *Twisted Cross: The German Christian Movement in the Third Reich.* Chapel Hill: University of North Carolina Press, 1996.

Cherry, Conrad, ed. *God's New Israel: Religious Interpretations of American Destiny.* Rev. ed. Chapel Hill: University of North Carolina Press, 1998.

Chin, Gabriel J., and Rose Cuison Villazor, eds. *The Immigration and Nationality Act of 1965: Legislating a New America.* New York: Cambridge University Press, 2015.

Clark, Victoria. *Allies for Armageddon: The Rise of Christian Zionism.* New Haven, CT: Yale University Press, 2007.

Cogley, Richard W. *John Eliot's Mission to the Indians Before King Philip's War.* Cambridge, MA: Harvard University Press, 1999.

Coogan, Michael D., and Cynthia R. Chapman. *The Old Testament: A Historical and Literary Introduction to the Hebrew Scriptures.* 4th ed. New York: Oxford University Press, 2018.

Ericksen, Robert P. *Theologians Under Hitler: Gerhard Kittel, Paul Althaus and Emanuel Hirsch.* New Haven, CT: Yale University Press, 1985.

Fea, John. *Was American Founded as a Christian Nation? A Historical Introduction.* Louisville, KY: Westminster John Knox, 2011.

Fitzmyer, Joseph A. *Romans: A New Translation with Introduction and Commentary.* New York: Doubleday, 1993.

Gitlin, Todd, and Liel Leibovitz. *The Chosen Peoples: America, Israel, and the Ordeals of Divine Election.* New York: Simon & Schuster, 2010.

Gorski, Philip. *American Covenant: A History of Civil Religion from the Puritans to the Present.* Princeton, NJ: Princeton University Press, 2017.

Green, Steven K. *Inventing a Christian America: The Myth of the Religious Founding.* New York: Oxford University Press, 2015.

Hanson, Paul D. *A Political History of the Bible in America.* Louisville, KY: Westminster John Knox, 2015.

Harkabi, Yehoshafat. *Israel's Fateful Hour*. Trans. Lenn Schramm. New York: Harper & Row, 1988.

Hughes, Richard T. *Christian America and the Kingdom of God*. Urbana: University of Illinois Press, 2009.

Hughes, Richard T. *Myths America Lives By*. Urbana: University of Illinois Press, 2003.

Hutchison, William R., and Hartmut Lehman, eds. *Many Are Chosen: Divine Election and Western Nationalism*. Minneapolis, MN: Fortress, 1994.

Kaminsky, Joel S. *Yet I Loved Jacob: Reclaiming the Biblical Concept of Election*. Nashville, TN: Abingdon, 2007.

Karpin, Michael, and Ina Friedman. *Murder in the Name of God: The Plot to Kill Yitzhak Rabin*. New York: Metropolitan, 1998.

Lohr, Joel N. *Chosen and Unchosen: Conceptions of Election in the Pentateuch and in Jewish-Christian Interpretation*. Winona Lake, IN: Eisenbrauns, 2009.

Lustick, Ian S. *For the Land and the Lord: Jewish Fundamentalism in Israel*. New York: Council on Foreign Relations, 1988.

O'Brien, Conor Cruise. *God Land: Reflections on Religions and Nationalism*. Cambridge, MA: Harvard University Press, 1988.

O'Brien, Jean M. *Dispossession by Degrees: Indian Land and Identity in Natick, Massachusetts, 1650–1790*. Cambridge, UK: Cambridge University Press, 1997.

Römer, Thomas. *The Invention of God*. Trans. Raymond Geuss. Cambridge, MA: Harvard University Press, 2015.

Rom-Shiloni, Dalit. *Exclusive Inclusivity: Identity Conflicts between the Exiles and the People Who Remained (6th–5th Centuries BCE)*. New York: Bloomsbury, 2013.

Rowley, H. H. *The Biblical Doctrine of Election*. London: Lutterworth, 1950.

Schor, Esther. *Emma Lazarus*. New York: Schocken, 2006.

Shahak, Israel, and Norton Mezvinsky. *Jewish Fundamentalism in Israel*. 2nd ed. London: Pluto, 2004.

Shenhav, Yehouda. *The Arab Jews: A Postcolonial Reading of Nationalism, Religion, and Ethnicity*. Stanford, CA: Stanford University Press, 2006.

Solberg, Mary M., ed. *A Church Undone: Documents from the German Christian Faith Movement 1932–1940*. Minneapolis: Fortress, 2015.

Wills, Lawrence M. *Not God's People: Insiders and Outsiders in the Biblical World*. Lanham, MD: Rowman & Littlefield, 2008.

Zakovitch, Yair. *Jacob: Unexpected Patriarch*. Trans. V. Zakovitch. New Haven, CT: Yale University Press, 2012.

INDEX

Aaron: Egyptian name of, 33; as
   first high priest, 32; rivalry with
   Moses, 22, 32; and worship of
   Yahweh, 37
abolition, and biblical view of
   slavery, 122
Abraham: as divinely chosen, 1, 11,
   17, 136n1; as immigrant, 115,
   152n1; in Jewish, Christian,
   and Muslim sacred texts, 89;
   migration of, 15, 16; sacrifice of
   son of, 90, 147n12
Abrahamic religions, 89, 90, 91,
   92
Adams, John, on American Revo-
   lution, 99
Akiba, Rabbi, on love of neighbor,
   154n36
Alexander the Great, in Judean
   history, 15
Al-Aqsa mosque, 90, 91, 92
Al-Quds, 90. See also Jerusalem
Allah, 146n3
Amalekites, Palestinian Arabs as,
   151n12
America, and chosenness, 2, 7, 8,
   93–103
American apartheid, 128
American Colony (Jerusalem), 111
American Colony Hotel, 152n20
American exceptionalism, 100, 101,
   102, 131

Americans, as new Israelites,
   102. See also America, and
   chosenness
Amir, Yigal, and assassination of
   Yitzhak Rabin, 110
Amos (prophet): inclusive view of
   Yahweh's concern, 58; on Yahweh's choice of Israel, 57
ancient Near Eastern writings, and
   interpretation of the Bible, 5
Anglican Church, Good Friday
   prayer of, 85, 86
Anglo-Saxon race, and American
   exceptionalism, 100, 101
anti-Semitism, 86, 146n30; and
   chosenness, 2; in Gospel of
   John, 83, 84
apocalyptic writings, and coming of
   Messiah to Jerusalem, 111–12
Apocrypha, 3, 141n10, 143n18
Arabs, ancient and modern, 108
Arabs, Palestinian: as Amalekites,
   151n12; as Canaanites, 151n12;
   descent from Canaanites, 108;
   displacement of, 123–24; as
   Ishmaelites, 114
Arafat, Yasser, 110
ark of the covenant, 53, 142n33
Artaxerxes I, and authorization to
   rebuild walls of Jerusalem, 68
Arthur, Chester A. (US president),
   127